What people are saying about …

hope in the eleventh hour

"*Hope in the Eleventh Hour* arrives precisely and powerfully into the deepest parts of our hurting hearts. This inspiring book connects with every emotion, from sweet smiles to tender tears. Sarah's eternal perspective shines a brilliant light on God's unchanging, inerrant Word and His forever promises to us and our loved ones who are Home."

Kathy Ireland, chair/CEO of
kathyirelandWorldwide

"My precious friend Sarah Berger faced the hardest thing a mother ever has to face on earth: the loss of a child. In *Hope in the Eleventh Hour*, she takes the reader along on her personal journey of loving her son who beat her to Heaven, highlighting the many ways God has spoken to her through His Word and in His tender touches. Beautifully written and hugely encouraging for everyone, this book will especially bring hope and healing to anyone who has endured the loss of a loved one."

Debbie Smith, wife of singer/songwriter
Michael W. Smith and mother of five

"Sarah takes us to a sacred place—into the soul of a mother who grieves and, in time, heals while navigating the valley of the shadow of death and into a trusting place of peace that could only be found in the Prince of Peace. Oh, to see the proud smile on Josiah's face as he cheers his brave mom on. Thank you, Sarah, for sharing the most precious places of your beautiful heart with us. I know it will be life-changing for everyone who reads your story."

Rebecca Nichols Alonzo, *New York Times*–bestselling author of *The Devil in Pew Number Seven*

"Sarah Berger's beautiful book, *Hope in the Eleventh Hour*, brims with authenticity from a woman who's traveled the incomprehensible and mystical road of grief. Biblically solid and filled with wisdom, her tender words will bring deep comfort to anyone dealing with loss, especially the loss of a child. Let her wisdom and personal experience shepherd you as you walk through the valley of the shadow of death, encouraging you to lean solidly on Jesus."

Kate Battistelli, author of *The God Dare* and *Growing Great Kids*

"My dear friend Sarah writes like she lives: with ferocity and truth. She has been the single most influential person in my own journey of losing my daughter to cancer; her words are wise, real, transformative. Upon finishing this book, I wanted to start all over again to make sure I didn't miss a thing! Full of heart, depth, and the mysteries of God, this book is necessary for any person who is ready to start healing from loss. Dive into this book and you will experience so much joy!"

Kate Merrick, mother of three, speaker, cofounder of Reality church, author of *And Still She Laughs* and *Here, Now*

"My dear friend Sarah Berger has penned a beautiful love letter to those suffering through the unbearable grief of having to release a child into Heaven. I witnessed Sarah's heartache firsthand as I mourned her precious Josiah right along with the family. With the Lord's help, she shepherds us through what seems to be an incurable loss and shows us all how to smile again."

Lisa Patton, bestselling author

"I have known Sarah as a friend, a pastor, and a mother. I remember when she sat waiting for her son Josiah to be healed and when she released him to be with the Lord. I then watched her sacred journey as she grieved the loss of his presence and her heart had to lean on God's arms for Josiah's memory. Her words are simple purity and fervent power. When you listen to her—and in this book read her thoughts and what she gleans from Scripture—you cannot help but want the One she is wholeheartedly devoted to. As Sarah unfolds her story, it is for us a divine encouragement to keep pressing on to that goal God has promised we would all find as we seek Him."

Rita Springer, artist, writer, singer

hope

in the

eleventh
hour

Sarah B. Berger

hope
in the
eleventh
hour

A Mother's Journey through Grief with Eternal Eyes

DAVID **C** COOK

transforming lives together

HOPE IN THE ELEVENTH HOUR
Published by David C Cook
4050 Lee Vance Drive
Colorado Springs, CO 80918 U.S.A.

Integrity Music Limited, a Division of David C Cook
Brighton, East Sussex BN1 2RE, England

The graphic circle C logo is a registered trademark of David C Cook.

Details in some stories have been changed to protect
the identities of the persons involved.

Library of Congress Control Number 2022938162
ISBN 978-0-8307-8425-7
eISBN 978-0-8307-8426-4

The Team: Susan McPherson, Stephanie Bennett, Renée
Chavez, James Hershberger, Susan Murdock
Cover Design: James Hershberger
Cover Art: Getty Images

Printed in the United States of America
First Edition 2022

1 2 3 4 5 6 7 8 9 10

071422

To my precious grandkids, Trinity, Maverick, Haven, Shiloh, Cohen, and all yet to come.

*You all bring Maw **SO** much joy.*

May you all continue to grow up with the wonder of meeting your Uncle Josiah one day in the place we call Home! He's a blast, and you are gonna love him so much!

To my dear parents, Al and Annie Benton, I honor you both. Dad, a World War II fighter pilot and cattle rancher, you taught us to live in wonder of creation. Mom, because you loved us so well, we have known how to love our husbands and children well also. You were married seventy-one years and held hands every day, and you both entered the Kingdom even as this manuscript took wings.

Well done, good and faithful servants (Matt. 25).

"Let not your heart be troubled; you believe in God, believe also in Me. In My Father's house are many mansions; if it were not so, I would have told you. I go to prepare a place for you. And if I go and prepare a place for you, I will come again and receive you to Myself; that where I am, there you may be also. And where I go you know, and the way you know."

John 14:1–4

contents

foreword

My first encounter with the death of an immediate family member was 11:08 p.m. on December 12, 2016. That's when my dad, who was unequivocally my favorite male on the planet, transitioned from earth to Heaven.

We had just celebrated his eightieth birthday, and that year he and my mom had enjoyed their fifty-fourth wedding anniversary. Dad had always been healthy, vibrant, and independent, and he jokingly bragged about being twenty years old four times. If you were to ask his age, he'd have declared himself to be eighty years young!

Everything my dad did was intentional, and each thing he did taught a lesson. On weekdays he led our family in 5:00 a.m. prayer. On Thursday nights we played tennis, and on Friday nights we went out to eat after the church service.

When I was a child, my dad taught my sisters and me to sing, and as we stood around the piano, he would give us our individual notes to make harmony. He also let us know that we didn't all have to do the same thing for something to work properly. If we were to actually sing our separate parts at the same time in the same key, then the song would be beautiful.

As I grew into an adult, my dad was always my rock and biggest supporter, and when some of my love relationships turned sour, he was the reason that I never said, "All men are ..."

He was a good father; he is a godly man. On more than one occasion, he'd say, "Death for the believer is not scary.... It's like walking from one room to another. It's a continuation of life beyond our imagination."

I miss him more than I can describe, and yet his words comfort me because they agree with the Scriptures. I can't wait to share with him the news about what's going on in my life and how Jesus is still showing Himself faithful. I can't wait to hear my dad fill me in on who he's met, who he's sung with, and what he's learned so far in Heaven!

It's a mixture of happiness and sorrow, but if they are sung together in the right key, then there is harmony.

Many of us have experienced the heartache and grief of someone transitioning out of our lives, but not everyone is qualified to speak, share, and teach on the subject like Sarah Berger is.

Sarah and her husband, Steve, were my pastors here in Tennessee for more than ten years. They have walked me through some of my toughest choices as well as celebrated and counseled me in some of my best decisions. Her godly perspective is not only insightful but healing.

The care we received from the church when my father passed into Glory was a true example of the Kingdom of God. The congregation reflected the grace of Steve and Sarah's leadership—leaders who had been dipped in grief. Like our Lord, who is acquainted with sorrow, they possess a godly perspective on death coupled with the utmost care, compassion, humility, and love. Steve and Sarah are not only close friends, but I consider them family as well.

You see, Sarah has publicly and privately walked through the corridors of what we commonly refer to as "loss." She has done so while clinging to Jesus, asking Him questions, and listening for answers. Sarah further explains that in many cases the word *loss* is not befitting. Our loved ones are actually "found" in the presence of God, behind the veil that separates this life from the next. Sometimes they may be given a glimpse into our world as a part of the great cloud of witnesses. Sometimes we are given a glimpse into theirs.

Death is a tender subject. When grief is observed rather than felt firsthand, it can be hard to know what to say to comfort someone. This book will not only help you say the right things but will also shift your thinking.

As sobering as it may sound, we will all experience what is generally considered the "loss" of a loved one, the transition of a believer in Christ. The length and magnitude of our pain may vary. And yet, as believers in Jesus, we are afforded a supernatural ingredient that not only keeps us afloat but also sets us apart. It's called hope.

Our hope springs from our faith in Christ and is rooted in His love. It changes our perspective and teaches us that those who have gone before us, no matter when they died, are actually enjoying unspeakable pleasures as we await our reunion.

I was thrilled to read this wonderful, grace-filled book, knowing that each page is bathed in honesty and prayer. And I am honored to introduce my friend and sister Sarah.

I assure you that the kindness, vulnerability, tone, and authenticity within these pages are indicative of the Sarah Berger I know and love. I can't wait for you to hear her story, glean from her wisdom, and gain comfort in your season of grief.

I am confident that by the end of the book, you will feel as if you have added a new friend, mentor, and sister to your life.

I pray that as you make room for Sarah to sit with you through the reading of this book, you will be encouraged and infused with the hope of the Holy Spirit in your eleventh hour.

My Redeemer Lives,
Nicole C. Mullen
Recording artist, author, speaker

acknowledgments

Thank You, Jesus, for sticking closer than a brother. For speaking my language and knowing what would make for my peace. For Your sacrifice that has made a way to reunite my family forever. For writing my story.

Thank you to my handsome and bravehearted hubby, Steve, for speaking truth over me for the past thirty-five years. For being resolved and unwavering for King Jesus even through the most excruciating pain. I love you so.

To my four incredible kids: You guys are my greatest victory! To see you all trusting Jesus with your lives and within your family units despite great sorrow can only be God. You are brave and good, and eternity with you all will be sheer bliss! Even so come, Lord Jesus.

To my precious and patient friend Jenn Hesse: Jesus gave me the best shot in the arm ever when He sent me you, dear Jenn. Thank you for working so tirelessly to help make my story clear. You are a gifted editor and faithful sis. Thank you for saying yes.

To my friend Katie Merrick: You'll never realize your portion in this manuscript being published. I kinda blame it on you and Jesus. You two make a great team.

To my agent, Teresa Evenson at William K Jensen: Everything about this book has been a surprise, and you are one of them! So much more than an agent, my sister and friend. Thank you for our long visits and great wisdom.

To my acquisition editor at DCC, Susan McPherson (Suz/Susan Mac): Yet another treasure and surprise. You too are a faithful sister and friend. I'm so grateful Jesus would provide such fellowship along the way.

Stephanie Bennett, friend, you're not just incredible at editing, you have the gift of encouragement. Thank you for your keen eye and kind words. You kept me going.

James Hershberger, how kind and patient you were through the cover design process. You went around and around with me, and in the end, Jesus gave you the perfect design.

The entire team at David C Cook has blown my mind. Everyone in unity. Everyone encouraging. Everyone displaying the fruit of the Spirit. Thank you all for gently walking me through the process. I am so grateful.

josiah's story

It was the summer of 2009. Josiah, our second of four children, was preparing for his freshman year at the University of Tennessee, Knoxville (UTK). One day he confessed, "I don't want to hurt anyone's feelings, but I am so ready to get outta here!" Josiah has always been full of adventure, and we knew he was ready to spread those wings and fly. Never would we have imagined that Josiah would be setting out on a heavenly journey—an adventure compared to none.

Earlier that summer, while praying for Josiah and his future, I'd sensed the Holy Spirit's nudging. He whispered to me that whatever Josiah wanted, whether big or small, I needed to say yes. I made an oath before the Lord to be obedient to His prompting. Saying yes to these little asks of Josiah was meant for my future healing. Only the Lord could have known how my heart would have been haunted by regret had I resisted these small favors.

So on August 11, when Josiah asked me to feed the dogs with him, I of course said yes. There were spiders in the shed where the food was kept, and Siah (as we call him) is afraid of spiders. He jokingly said, "MOJ [mother of Josiah], will you go with me?" We had the most precious moment while walking back to the house, arms wrapped around each other. I realized that this would be the last time we fed the dogs together until Christmas—as he was leaving in just four days for UTK and schedules were busy—but he said, "No, Mom, I'll be back for fall break!" We hugged and laughed, and I assured him that I totally understood his excitement about leaving for college.

Later that night, about 10:45, Josiah came downstairs and said he was going to meet some friends at Sonic. It was later than he originally thought they would be meeting, but he still wanted to go, as some of his friends were leaving for college the next day. When I tried to give him an out, Josiah replied, "What kind of friend would I be if I didn't go?" That is the kind of guy Josiah is—a very intentional, loyal friend. I told him to come over and give me a kiss on the cheek, which he gladly did. We said our "I love yous," and then he left, drove down a familiar country road, and had an inexplicable single-car accident.

To be true, and still to this day, these are hard words to speak, but I must share. Within twenty minutes of Josiah walking out our door, he was walking through *the* door into his eternal Home. In literally the eleventh hour, on the evening of August 11, Josiah launched into his eternal adventure. Thrust into forever, for-ever. Josiah's beautiful tent, his temporal body, was kept on life support as thousands prayed for a miracle.

While in the hospital room with my son, I found myself saying things to him that were birthed out of my knowing that our Father God loves my son and that Father God loves our family. I told my Siah to do what the Father said—that only He knew what was right. The kind people at Vanderbilt Hospital had never seen such an outpouring from the community. People from around our immediate area and beyond stayed the night on the floor of a conference room, prayer-walked around the hospital, and worshipped on their knees, while others held prayer vigils at the church campus. The body of Christ was pleading for a Lazarus miracle, but all the while, I knew Josiah was already in the presence of the King.

Three days later, August 14, on Josiah's nineteenth birthday, we released his physical body to fulfill his own desire to be an organ donor. I still with absolute clarity recall the day Josiah came home from the DMV at age eighteen and excitedly shared with me that he had signed up to be a donor. I had turned my head to hide my eyes welling with tears as I told him how proud I was of him. Since I knew of Josiah's desire, I had assumed Steve knew also. I thought we were reasoning with whether we were going to comply with that final decision. However, Steve wasn't aware of Josiah's decision and was taken aback at the hospital when he was informed of Josiah's wishes.

In those final minutes with our son here on earth, we'd hoped for the miracle of Josiah's physical healing, but God in His sovereignty was showing His divine intimacy by giving us peace that passes understanding. He was there with us, in the eleventh hour, the last minute, in His painful and perfect timing, providing every detail we needed to quite literally give us our next breath. Ultimately, we followed through on Josiah's wishes, and through his gift of life, he saved the lives of five individuals and changed the lives of seventy-seven people. This list has only increased as Josiah's life on earth and in Heaven has continued to challenge and woo people from all over the world into a relationship with Christ. It was bitter and sweet of

our God to set things up since the beginning of time to fulfill all
Josiah had to give on this side of Heaven.

It's now been eleven years since our son Josiah David left for Heaven.
It is a surreal thing to even speak. *Eleven years?* How can that be?
I can still recall Josiah's distinct voice. Nothing about my son has
been forgotten, as it seems a mother never loses these memories. I am
confident I will have no problem distinguishing Josiah's voice from
the roaring crowd on that great day. But alas, eleven years it has been
since I last heard his audible voice.

> Ask the hard questions,
> and be fully honest with the
> God who knows all things.
> Nothing is hidden from Him.

Could you graciously lean in just a bit? I invite you to peer into
my heart before turning another page. I have walked with the Lord
for forty years now, and although I would never esteem myself a
Bible scholar, I have enjoyed the richness of its study and hold the
Word up as my standard. All that said, I am a product of the Jesus
Movement, and my spiritual DNA speaks to the inerrancy of the
Word, coupled with the balance of believing in all the Holy Spirit

offers. My husband says it best, and I adamantly agree: we want everything Scripture affords us, but nothing more. In other words: holy fire, but not strange fire!

I know that you are also grieving—perhaps feeling disillusionment and disappointment along with so many other emotions from a child or loved one going to Heaven before you—and you're wondering how to carry on. If you'll stick with me, I will share insight as to how God will provide for you and be near to you in the midst of your own brokenness. I'll walk you through the milestone lessons God has taught me over the last eleven years and share what I've gleaned. I promise, there are life-giving stories here that will help you see God and remind you that you're never ever alone.

The Holy Spirit has shown me that He, the God of *all* comfort, has been intent on answering all my intimate and at times bold questions about my son as He has tended to my heart. He wants open dialogue, mothers. Ask the hard questions, and be fully honest with the God who knows all things. Nothing is hidden from Him.

God will speak through whatever means He deems profitable—an injured bird, a piece of art, a hug from a random stranger, a dream, a vision, or the time of day—and He will confirm it through His Word. He is always speaking, and we need to pay attention.

Within these pages, I'm simply sharing my intimate story. I bear my soul to offer a glimpse of how the Lord might possibly be speaking to you also. Tears can at times blind us to the nearness and comfort He offers, and I don't want you to miss a thing. In my experience, the Lord has used dreams, symbolism, riddles, analogies, time, and numbers—coupled with lots of biblical context—to capture my heart and attention. Throughout my walk, He has set

me on treasure hunts through the Bible to find my answers. He has
spoken things that were out of the box—but of course, within biblical boundaries—things I never could have imagined.

> The way He has spoken to me
> might open your eyes to see His
> nearness and His concern for
> those who are brokenhearted.

God has been my nearest companion and strongest ally as I've
walked through deep loss and unimaginable grief. I would never
assume everyone's experiences are the same as mine. God is much
bigger than that, and He has His own unique way with each of His
kids. I do hope, however, that the way He has spoken to me might
open your eyes to see His nearness and His concern for those who
are brokenhearted. He is "near to those who have a broken heart, and
saves such as have a contrite spirit" (Ps. 34:18). *Near* means "near,"
but there is even more meaning in the Hebrew word—*qārôb*—used
in this verse. It also means "allied"![1] He is on our side, working with
us toward hope, peace, and, ultimately, victory.

> Therefore we do not lose heart. Even though our
> outward man is perishing, yet the inward man is
> being renewed day by day. For our light affliction,
> which is but for a moment, is working for us a far
> more exceeding and eternal weight of glory, while

we do not look at the things which are seen, but at the things which are not seen. For the things which are seen are temporary, but the things which are not seen are eternal. (2 Cor. 4:16–18)

For God so loved the world that He gave His only begotten Son, that whoever believes in Him should not perish but have everlasting life. For God did not send His Son into the world to condemn the world, but that the world through Him might be saved. (John 3:16–17)

chapter 1

God's immediate comfort

God knew when He would receive Josiah; our son's days were written in His book before he was even born (see Ps. 139:16). In my experience, the hazy, thick moments of those last minutes and first hours, when the comfort of God is moving you and compelling you forward, are confounding. He gives the words and answers when your own thoughts are not seemingly connected. He is there, seeing to it all, whatever the "all" may be. Things hidden, things unknown, things assumed—He saw to them all.

Looking back, the best description I can give of that time is of feeling blindfolded, not knowing the way but having the Lord Himself holding my shoulders from behind and turning me at every corner, guiding me through the valley of death itself. We didn't know how to navigate this path, but the God of all comfort was with us.

He was clearly in the planning of an incredible gift to our grieving family that began a year or so *before* Josiah's accident. Some folks from church were venturing out with the dream of building a boys' home in the Dominican Republic (DR), and their project was well on its way when Josiah left for Heaven. When the architect asked the family what the name of the home would be, the answer came quickly to them: "Josiah's House." We were surprised and overwhelmed. We knew somehow in the heavenlies that our Josiah would love it too.

The following spring break, some of Josiah's high school friends inquired about going on a mission trip instead of doing their usual plans. Their lives had been rocked, and they knew they needed to help others. So we decided to lead a crew of kids to the DR to work together on Josiah's House. We painted, we cried, we laughed, we read the Word—and we did it together. The house is now a campus that offers a loving home environment for boys in San Pedro, DR. Josiah's legacy of service, love, and encouragement lives on through the ministry that bears his name.

In the years since Josiah left for the Kingdom, the Lord has continued to show His comfort and presence in the most astonishing ways. Our self-published book, *Have Heart*, which is full of treasures the Lord gave us within the first months of Josiah's leaving, has reached countless people walking the same tender road of grief. We continue to hear from many, but especially parents, about how it is the most life-giving book on grief they have read. I suppose it's simply because of the truth of God's Word that it holds and the deep look at eternal life that it gives, written by folks who were in the throes of grief and living it out firsthand.

So why did I decide to write this second book? First, I wrote it in flat-out obedience to what I believe God asked me to do. Within these pages, you will find the story of the disobedience I walked in for some time before I finally said yes to His prompting. Writing seemed like a daunting task, until finally … it wasn't. Little did I know He was reminding my soul of His faithfulness. I am astonished at the great lengths He went to, to minister truth and healing to me. Now I live free from the regret of wonder—wondering if it was in fact His voice.

Second, I've written this book for my grandkids. If they are the only ones to ever hear these stories, I would say, "That is enough!" My prayer is that their little childlike hearts will be shaped for eternity and that they will look toward Heaven with excitement and wonder. I pray that they will all trust Jesus for salvation and live in expectation of His soon return, just like their Maw, Papa, and parents do. As Luke 12:37–38 says:

> Blessed are those servants whom the master, when he comes, will find watching. Assuredly, I say to you that he will gird himself and have them sit down to eat, and will come and serve them. And if he should come in the second watch, or come in the third watch, and find them so, blessed are those servants.

Finally, I wrote to prompt all of us who believe in Christ for our salvation to make much of Heaven as our eternal Home. Let us not tuck Heaven away in some corner but rather look forward with joy to our true Home. I pray that we will openly and with freedom mention our loved ones now living in Heaven as if they are alive, because in fact, they *are* alive.

In this moment, I pose the question: Does it bring you life when I say, "Your loved one in Heaven is alive"? He or she is not a *was* but a very alive *is*! Josiah is still my son. He is still a friend. Josiah is alive! Why do we refer to saints by saying, "He was such a good son," or "She was such a good friend"? *They still are*—only living it out on the other side of a very thin veil.

You've probably noted at this point that I never refer to Josiah as dead or in the past tense but as alive in Heaven. Possibly you thought I'd made a few grammatical errors in these initial pages. Nope, I am being very intentional. You see, our family quickly learned that referring to a saint living in Heaven as dead didn't make sense—not biblical sense, that is. (We're going to read chapter and verse to further drive this point home in chapter 4.)

This book you hold is full of stories that God has woven into my life along this path over the last decade. He has been so kind to shepherd this mom through the toughest terrain I could ever have imagined. He has kept me steady, using His staff to nudge me should I near a dangerous edge. He has gently held me with His every word, because His words in these moments are a literal source of life.

> Uphold me according to Your word, that I may live;
> And do not let me be ashamed of my hope.
> (Ps. 119:116)

Our omnipresent (present everywhere at the same time) and omniscient (all-knowing, all-wise, all-seeing) God plans out our days, and we have the opportunity to stay in step with Him (not jumping ahead, missing Him, or lagging behind). Let's pursue Him and say aloud to the Lord, "I don't want to miss a thing!"

I hope you receive fresh insight into God's comfort. I pray you will have the most joy-filled, profound moments of revelation. Whether looking back on the road you've already walked or seeing with more clarity what He may be saying to you now, know this: He is the God of all comfort. He is speaking to us within our deepest grief and possibly in ways to which we have been blind. He is reaching out to us in intimate, astounding ways.

> I know you are grieving—and you're wondering how you're going to carry on. But hang with me. God is ever near.

While going through Josiah's personal things after his passing, we found a letter he had written to himself the summer after his freshman year at Franklin High School in Franklin, Tennessee. In it, Josiah shared how the people he had met that year had all given him a special something and how very much it meant to him. Indulge this mom as I share some of Siah's personal words to "self":

> I just had one of the best prayer/cry sessions I've
> ever had. Actually, it was THE best. I pray that

God will help me be strong and not stray from being myself and fulfilling my goals for Him and myself. I can do this. At Franklin, I hope I can make a difference. That's what I really want to do. Be felt, like I feel people. I guess this feeling is love. Not marital love, but a love nonetheless. Or maybe it is an appreciation. An amazing high of appreciation and thankfulness of what I am feeling. I am so thankful and appreciative of what I have gotten from the students and teachers at Franklin. I will NEVER forget the people that have touched my life from FHS, The Happiest Place on Earth.

Yes, these are Josiah's own words. He fulfilled his mission. His prayers were answered, and he made a profound difference in all our lives. Now the legacy continues.

I know you are grieving—and you're wondering how you're going to carry on. But hang with me. God is ever near, and He's not going to leave you. What's more, He will take care of you during this painful season—and always. We'll talk more about that in the chapters to come. If you are ready, grab my hand and let's go!

Reflection

In Matthew 13:10–11, the disciples came and asked Jesus, "'Why do You speak to [the people] in parables?' He answered and said to them, 'Because it has been given to you to know the mysteries of the kingdom of heaven, but to them it has not been given.'" Commentators say His purpose was to reveal and conceal.

Are there things the Lord has been showing you that others have not seen? Has He spoken through His very Word things you've never understood before? Take a moment to journal questions and/or answers that He has stirred even within this first chapter. Ask the Lord for His help because He is our helper.

> But the Helper, the Holy Spirit whom the Father will send in My name, He will teach you all things, and bring to your remembrance all things that I said to you. (John 14:26)

chapter 2

it's about time

So teach us to number our days,
That we may gain a heart of wisdom.

Psalm 90:12

In 2011, almost two years after Josiah left for Heaven, our church experienced what most would consider a "good" problem. Between our two Sunday morning services, there was gridlock in the parking lot. As the pastors met, the remedy seemed simple. We needed an extra ten minutes to get the parking lot emptied to make room for the people coming to the second service—only ten minutes. With that, my husband and senior pastor, Steve Berger, tenderly suggested 11:11 as the start time. All who were there in the meeting knew that eleven minutes past the eleventh hour held special significance not only to the Berger family but to many who loved Josiah. At every mention of 11:11, it was impossible not to think of our son in Heaven.

You'll remember that Josiah flew Home to eternity on August 11 during the 11th hour. Not only that, but during Josiah's time on earth, 11:11 was a prompt that Josiah had frequently used to brighten someone's day. After Josiah left for eternity, his friend Marybeth mentioned that he would frequently text her at 11:11 to say, "Make a wish!" After she brought it to our attention, we discovered that this was another sweet something he carried out for more than one of his friends. It was just one of his many gestures to make everyone feel special and appreciated.

More than a sentimental time we set for our second Sunday service, 11:11 was a number that God had been using in my own personal prayer life, although I hadn't realized it yet. Often, He spoke to me through the recalling of Scripture verses, but I'm not so great at memorizing their locations. (If it's possible, I may have a form of dyslexia when it comes to numbers; I've struggled with numbers my entire life.)

I had been praying the following prayer time and time again, and the passages in it had become some of my go-to verses that were written across my heart. Even though I was completely ignorant of the source, I had been praying Luke 11:11–13 and 2 Corinthians 12:9. In my immediate hours of desperation, barely able to breathe, my prayer looked like this:

> Father God, I know You are a good God. I know You give good gifts. You're not going to give me a stone when I ask for bread. I do not even know what to ask for, but every good thing that I need to survive this pain, I'm begging for now. You say Your grace is sufficient, and I know You are not a liar, so I ask for more of Your grace, more of Your strength. I am asking for all You have for me, Lord, and to protect

me from all that is not of You! Open my eyes and
ears, because I cannot bear to miss a thing.

Several months later, although I was still mourning deeply and
losing thousands of tears daily, in a pivotal moment I had a sudden
knowing that we were going to make it. Folks around us would
gingerly remark that we were walking our grief out well. This was a
strange statement to me; to word it better, what they were really saying was, "You still believe!" Of course we did, but it made me ask the
Lord, *Why is our journey different from others? What is the standout
reason that we still trust and love You and each other?*

It is said that these great trials can make one bitter or better, and
I suppose we chose better. We understood that in this life we are
guaranteed tribulation. We didn't want the answer that was given,
but we trusted that "whatever was right, we would receive" (adapted
from Matthew 20, which we will discuss momentarily). We are not
promised all "good" days based on our commitment and years of
serving Christ. Parents suffer these losses all day every day around
the globe. So we didn't ask, "Why us?" but rather, "Why not us?"

It made me think of a conversation in Matthew 19 between
Jesus and His disciples after Peter asked a raw, honest question about
rewards:

> Then Peter answered and said to Him, "See, we
> have left all and followed You. *Therefore what shall
> we have?*"
>
> So Jesus said to them, "Assuredly I say to you,
> that in the regeneration, when the Son of Man sits

on the throne of His glory, you who have followed
Me will also sit on twelve thrones, judging the
twelve tribes of Israel. And everyone who has left
houses or brothers or sisters or father or mother or
wife or children or lands, for My name's sake, shall
receive a hundredfold, and inherit eternal life. But
many who are first will be last, and the last first."
(vv. 27–30)

Jesus' answer is, of course, perfect, as He saw way past the
immediate question into the heart of the matter and reassured Peter
and the other disciples that their reward would be unbelievable.
They would receive a hundredfold of what they sacrificed on earth
and inherit eternal life.

Our observant Jesus noted that the crew didn't react with the
expected gratefulness at the mention of the last item of compensa-
tion. You see, the last thing Jesus mentioned was actually the highest
in value. Eternal life is certainly worthy of tears and gratitude at the
mere mention; the thing the disciples overlooked should have been
the first and primary thing that mattered—the last shall be first!

What does the above conversation have to do with me? Well,
Peter knew the pain of leaving everything to follow Christ and
wanted to know if it would be worth it. What was in it for him?
What's in it for us? This passage answered the question of my heart,
Is this deep pain going to be worth it?

Our eleventh-hour miracle was having the security of knowing
that our son was experiencing his hundredfold reward—and in a
land far beyond that which we experience here. I know this may be

difficult to hear. I beg you to stay with me, because amid your great sorrow, as you agree with what is scripturally sound, you can trust God's sovereignty and ask your questions; you *will* see Him. He will answer, and in your eleventh hour, you will hear Him speak. It may not be what you expected, but in the end, you will find yourself richer for having trusted in Him.

What do I mean by "the eleventh hour"? Well, the eleventh hour holds much significance in our personal story, and through study of the Word, we see it holds significance for us all. The phrase "the eleventh hour" is scriptural. It's curious how so many of our cultural phrases come straight from the Word, yet we seldom know the real weight they carry. This teaching has the potential to bring those of us who are suffering much comfort if we are courageous enough to receive it.

Let's look at Matthew 20:1–16, a parable of Jesus, for additional insight:

> For the kingdom of heaven is like a landowner who went out early in the morning to hire laborers for his vineyard. Now when he had agreed with the laborers for a denarius a day, he sent them into his vineyard. And he went out about the third hour and saw others standing idle in the marketplace, and said to them, "You also go into the vineyard, and whatever is right I will give you." So they went. Again he went out about the sixth and the ninth hour, and did likewise. And about the eleventh hour he went out and found others

standing idle, and said to them, "Why have you been standing here idle all day?" They said to him, "Because no one hired us." He said to them, "You also go into the vineyard, and whatever is right you will receive."

So when evening had come, the owner of the vineyard said to his steward, "Call the laborers and give them their wages, beginning with the last to the first." And when those came who were hired about the eleventh hour, they each received a denarius. But when the first came, they supposed that they would receive more; and they likewise received each a denarius. And when they had received it, they complained against the landowner, saying, "These last men have worked only one hour, and you made them equal to us who have borne the burden and the heat of the day." But he answered one of them and said, "Friend, I am doing you no wrong. Did you not agree with me for a denarius? Take what is yours and go your way. I wish to give to this last man the same as to you. Is it not lawful for me to do what I wish with my own things? Or is your eye evil because I am good?" So the last will be first, and the first last. For many are called, but few chosen.

Within the parable of the laborers in the vineyard, there is a heart issue being addressed—correcting the perspective of what holds true worth in the Kingdom. Jesus in His all-knowingness seized the moment to make His answer in Matthew 19 even clearer. He extended His explanation beyond the reward issue and into the heart issue.

You see, the only workers who were guaranteed an amount of money were those who arrived to work first. The grandest reward was what the landowner (or Jesus) sealed with the first-hour laborers. He guaranteed them each a denarius, representing eternal life. This payment (of eternal life) was going to be distributed evenly among the laborers simply because they had said yes to the work. It wasn't given because of the number of hours spent in the vineyard as much as their believing that the payment was a sure thing and trusting the landowner at his word.

After that, the laborers who came during the third, sixth, and finally the eleventh hours were all simply told, "Whatever is right I will give you" (v. 4). These latecomers, I imagine, were curious, as they were brought into the workforce so late in the day. Why the invite? What help would they be? Nonetheless, they labored and in the end were also met with an amazing, blessed denarius.

The laborers who had come first and worked the entire day felt they were entitled to more than those who had worked a partial day. They were given what the landowner guaranteed, and in the end, he called them out after he found them complaining.

The equal wage disbursed shows us so much about the mind of Christ. One, He is "no respecter of persons" (Acts 10:34 KJV), meaning He doesn't care about rank. Two, Jesus loves us all so much that He will offer an equal wage to everyone who believes—whether they have been at this Christian thing for hours or years. Why can't we celebrate and be overjoyed at the gift these latecomers are also given?

I see an enormous issue being addressed in these passages. This may be difficult for some of us in the midst of our suffering, but I beg you to try. We can see thoughts of *I deserve more!* (or, perhaps, *I deserve better*). Stay with me, because it's similar to *I have served You faithfully for years, Lord, and this is how You reward me? The loss of my son? The loss of a relationship? The loss of employment?*

This gets to the heart of entitlement and earthly rewards. Entitlement is contrary to the core of Christianity. Here on earth, we are called to die to self, to serve and not be served, and to set our sights on Heaven. We are given peace, hope, and everything else the Spirit offers us to get through our mission.

In certain seasons, we are walking in so much favor that we can slip into comfort and, rather than appreciate it as a unique and divine season of blessing, we grow to expect it. We may feel like it is deserved because of our efforts. Be thankful. Enjoy the moments when everything is going smoothly, and give thanks to God for His provision, but do not build your foundation on the sand. If you do, then when storms rise, your house will fall (see Matt. 7:26–27). Trials will come, and there are certainly ones that cut to the core, but He is with us, offering a window into His heart. Oh, if only we would come look.

The point to remember is this: everyone got a denarius, or eternal life. In the end, all that really matters is bringing as many into the Kingdom as possible. But hear my heart: your loved one has made it Home. It is all about Home—not making less of eternity but more.

I want to pause for a moment to make much of Heaven and its inhabitants in order to dispel any fear or anguish. We know well the Enemy of our souls is a liar and has no regard for a vulnerable, broken heart. Perhaps you're thinking, *My baby was never given the opportunity to work for the landowner or to say yes to Jesus.* Sister, if you had a baby that passed in utero, during infancy, or as a small child, let's end the lies. Your baby is alive and experiencing joy unimaginable in Heaven. You are that child's mom, and you will one day be reunited.

Now, dear one, this is so incredibly tender, but Jesus wants to touch your pain too. If perhaps you terminated your baby's life here on earth before birth, please know that Jesus in His goodness has welcomed that little one Home. Your child is whole, well, and experiencing beautiful eternal life. And you, upon receiving Christ as Savior, have also been given eternal life and the opportunity of a sacred do-over of life with your child in Heaven. Even now, in my mind's eye, I can see hundreds of thousands of mothers running with inexpressible joy toward their children on that great day. Eternal life, redemption, and the most tear-filled, joyful reunion ever.

> And God will wipe away every tear from their eyes;
> there shall be no more death, nor sorrow, nor crying. There shall be no more pain, for the former
> things have passed away. (Rev. 21:4)

Fellow sojourners, receive this encouragement. Don't complain and misunderstand the Landowner as somehow stingy. He sacrificed His life to give you and your loved one that one thing that matters most: life forever! "For the wages of sin is death, but the gift of God is eternal life in Christ Jesus our Lord" (Rom. 6:23). You cannot save yourself, "for by grace you have been saved through faith, and that not of yourselves; it is the gift of God, not of works, lest anyone should boast" (Eph. 2:8–9).

When I reflect on Peter and his questions and statements, I realize how much he was ministered to, especially after he had betrayed Christ three times—and so soon after he boldly stated he never would. I imagine that when Peter reflected on the parable of those eleventh-hour workers, he had a far deeper understanding—even appreciation—of how it felt to be so undeserving and yet be given so much. In my journey, I've found that the folks who have walked away from Christ when times got tough are those who expected more. Possibly they read over the forewarnings of trial and tribulation, never imagining that they might one day be face to face with the worst imaginable.

We all at one time or another can find ourselves arguing with a sovereign God, telling Him that somehow we deserve more than the eleventh-hour workers. But friend, isn't that because we don't fully grasp the weight and glory of the gift of eternal life? If you've raised your fist toward the Lord, shouting, "How could You, God? I didn't deserve this blow. Why me?" possibly, my fellow sojourner, you have not grasped the glory of eternity and how it is the most treasured of all rewards. That "wage" is priceless!

Paul says in Romans 8:18 that he considers "the sufferings of this present time are not worthy to be compared with the glory which shall be revealed in us." He is speaking about eternity! This incredibly devastating season of grief so pales in comparison to eternity in Heaven, especially an eternity with our loved ones in Christ. But how do we even grasp this? How is it possible to make this suffering become small when it seems to consume our beings? We believe the Word. We speak it back to our Creator. We tell Him what His Word says and stand on the hope and enormity of eternity. Heaven is far better, and it will be worth it all.

One day, while reading through the book of John, a statement Jesus made leaped off the page. John 14:28 says, "You have heard Me say to you, 'I am going away and coming back to you.' If you loved Me, you would rejoice because I said, 'I am going to the Father,' for My Father is greater than I." That line struck me to the core. The Lord was challenging me to a heart check. He spoke these words in a gentle and convincing tone. "Do you trust Me or not? Do you love Josiah?"

"Yes, Father, I love Josiah!"

"If you love him, you should be happy that he has come to Me. Sarah, I know this grief is so deep there are no words to describe it. Now, take your focus off the despair you feel and magnify eternity. Make much of Heaven. Josiah loves it here." In my mind, I could see Josiah saying, *"Mom, I know you love me. Please be happy that I am Home."*

Friend, if you are bitter toward the Lord, disappointed in what you received, please take a moment to repent and find Him there. Allow Him to heal your broken heart and release you from the prison of bitterness that binds you. He is near and He will bring you through. It is said of the Lord that He is seldom early but never late. Hold on for His eleventh-hour remedy.

Fast-forward to March 2016. I was sitting in our Wednesday morning ladies' Bible study. The teacher was closing her study when she mentioned Luke 11:11. My chin immediately lifted from taking notes as she began to read the verses:

> If a son asks for bread from any father among you, will he give him a stone? Or if he asks for a fish, will he give him a serpent instead of a fish? Or if he asks for an egg, will he offer him a scorpion? If you then, being evil, know how to give good gifts to your children, how much more will your heavenly Father give the Holy Spirit to those who ask Him! (Luke 11:11–13)

My heart skipped a beat, and I felt joy filling me up! Beyond what God had already revealed about His eleventh-hour comfort and grace, I'd always felt there had to be more to 11:11 specifically, and this was it. You see, only the Father would have known that these very verses were the ones I'd prayed over and over as I knelt on the floor in a million tears.

In context, Luke 11:1–13 is chock-full of a noticeably clear and continued theme. The Father wants us to ask! He wants conversation and relationship. He wants us in every season of our lives to be ready and longing to ask Him the big, the small, the raw questions. Just like Peter, ask whatever is on your mind, even if you get exposed by His answer. Ask for daily bread. Ask for forgiveness. Ask for a loaf for a friend. Ask, seek, knock, and keep on knocking until the door is opened, and never ever stop. Let's read the passage together:

> And it came to pass, that, as he was praying in a certain place, when he ceased, one of his disciples said unto him, Lord, teach us to pray, as John also taught his disciples.
>
> And he said unto them, When ye pray, say, Our Father which art in heaven, Hallowed be thy name. Thy kingdom come. Thy will be done, as in heaven, so in earth.
>
> Give us day by day our daily bread.
>
> And forgive us our sins; for we also forgive every one that is indebted to us. And lead us not into temptation; but deliver us from evil.
>
> And he said unto them, Which of you shall have a friend, and shall go unto him at midnight, and say unto him, Friend, lend me three loaves;
>
> For a friend of mine in his journey has come to me, and I have nothing to set before him?
>
> And he from within shall answer and say, Trouble me not: the door is now shut, and my children are with me in bed; I cannot rise and give thee.

I say unto you, Though he will not rise and give him, because he is his friend, yet because of his importunity he will rise and give him as many as he needeth.

And I say unto you, Ask, and it shall be given you; seek, and ye shall find; knock, and it shall be opened unto you.

For every one that asketh receiveth; and he that seeketh findeth; and to him that knocketh it shall be opened.

If a son shall ask bread of any of you that is father, will he give him a stone? or if he asks a fish, will he for a fish give him a serpent?

Or if he shall ask an egg, will he offer him a scorpion?

If ye then, being evil, know how to give good gifts unto your children: how much more shall your heavenly Father give the Holy Spirit to them that ask him? (KJV)

It is so important to note that at the top of the chapter, Jesus is teaching us how to pray. In His brilliance, He lets us know via the parable that He wants us to ask the most outlandish of things. Even questions that may seem rude or ignorant. I mean, who asks his neighbor for three loaves of bread at *midnight*, and not even for himself, but for some guests who have arrived? But the neighbor gets his friend the loaves because of his importunity. Let's look at the definition of that word:

im-por-tu-ni-ty (n.)

    persistence, especially to the point of annoyance[1]

My asking and begging may have appeared the same to an onlooker, but I am not one to ever get too caught up in what others think, so I asked and asked again, "Father God, I know You are a good Father, and You would not give me a stone when I need bread! I know You! You want me to ask, and so here I am, asking. I need You, Holy Spirit. I need more of everything You have for me. I do not want anything apart from You!"

I have found it is far better to walk with Jesus *through* the grief than to bury it with food, alcohol, or other distractions. All these options are counterfeits compared to the only source that can genuinely touch the pain: Jesus. No placebo, no counterfeit, no lie! Taking time to grieve at His feet, sitting in His presence, and giving our burdens to Him is *the way* to healing (see John 14:6).

I knew my good God and His character well before being thrust into deep grief. I knew He delights in His children trusting Him. He invites our conversation and questions! It's His choice to answer or not. But I knew I must trust that, in His sovereignty, He had not only my best in mind but also His best for my son Josiah and our dear family.

> I have found it is far better to walk with Jesus *through* the grief than to bury it with food, alcohol, or other distractions.

I so distinctly remember praying, "Father, You are a good God, and I know You love when I ask outlandish things. Please, merciful God, show me what You deem good for me to know! Withhold and set a boundary around me from anything that is not of You!" I knew His grace was sufficient, and I would hold Him to that very promise when my heart was in a million pieces. I continued, "Father, I know You are good. You love me; You love my family; You love Josiah! You say your grace is sufficient, and so I trust You to give us everything we need to survive this devastation. I want everything you have for me. Speak!" And He did—and He continues to speak to me this day. Luke 11:11 was His word for me on August 11, 2009, and it is His word for me today!

As I listened at our women's Bible study, the Lord confirmed again that He was there all along. Romans 8:26 states, "Now in the same way the Spirit also helps our weakness; for we do not know what to pray for as we should, but the Spirit Himself intercedes for us with groanings too deep for words" (NASB). The study of Luke 11 was a full-circle moment. It took me back to the prayers from early in my grief walk, which in turn created a well of gratefulness as I recounted how lovingly God had fed me daily manna. The Holy Spirit had interceded for me with incomprehensible words that drew me along the path with Him to this point. He gave me the words to pray. The very Scripture I needed to be asking. In my weakness, He saw to it.

Then, in a moment of clarity, I realized that it had been seven years and seven months since Josiah had left for Heaven. How like God to drop this reminder of His perfect gifts and perfect timing by using the number seven—signifying completion and wholeness.

It felt like the closing of a loop—the finishing of an open-ended question that came to mind every now and again. He answered just when He deemed it right. Just in time, if you will. His intricacies are all over your story too. Start opening your eyes to see them.

As if that weren't enough, God was about to drop more bread-crumbs onto my path to confirm His will. After my discovery at Bible study, I called the teacher and we talked through the sudden insight Jesus had given me. I also privately shared how I thought God had been telling me for months to write these stories to help others see Him in the midst of their grief. I had been praying through it, seeking clarity, and asking, "Is that really You, God, or am I imagining it?" Without hesitation the teacher replied, "Sarah! It's about time!"

These are the stories of how the Lord has deposited pieces of His truth for me along the way, His "bread of life," to pick up and partake of. As I have eaten the Father's manna, my worship has grown deeper in His presence. He has driven out devastation and replaced it with sound understanding. In His perfect time and in my desperate place, He was there, and He still remains. My roots in Jesus Christ are far deeper, and my heart's desire to glorify His name has only increased.

Father God, I pray this book of stories You have given me and for me will work to heal hearts and encourage others to listen along their way, to pay attention to their surroundings, and to open their eyes to the manna on their paths that leads to restoration, hope, and eternal life. Because we trust You and You are a good God, we are believing for eleventh-hour miracles full of Your grace and comfort. Please provide our next breath on this uphill journey through grief and pain. Like a holy "bread trail" along the way, lead us on, Father God! It's about time!

Reflection

In John 6:67, Jesus asks the disciples, "Do you also want to go away?" My hope would be that we would answer as Simon Peter did: "Lord, to whom shall we go? You have the words of eternal life" (v. 68). The world offers plenty of comforts, diversions, and avenues for processing grief, but the longer we meander, the more we muddy our grief walk and multiply our heartache.

Ask the Lord to reveal if you've possibly strayed from Him. Are you falling into one hole after another? List each one. Call them all out and confess them before your loving God.

Father, I know You are the only one with words of eternal life. Strengthen my heart and mind to look only to You in my time of need.

chapter 3

one body, one bread

For we, though many, are one bread and one
body; for we all partake of that one bread.

1 Corinthians 10:17

Within a few days of Josiah leaving for Heaven, as days and nights were blurred in grief, the idea of the "body of Christ" began running through my mind. For many of us, it can take several attempts before we realize the Holy Spirit is trying to say something. At last, I realized it was the Holy Spirit beckoning me to take a step, leading me into an important truth He needed to settle in my heart immediately.

This first revelation would prove to be pivotal because it set the standard and became my go-to time and time again. The Spirit's first of many life-giving bits of truth on this path through grief coaxed me forward into His comfort and hope.

In my heart, a reasoning began between God and me. "Sarah, think about the body of Christ. Would I cut off My arm? Would I cut off My leg?"

"No, Lord," I replied.

"Nor have I cut off Josiah from the body of Christ."

I knew in an instant what Father God was wanting to communicate to this grieving mom. Out of His own hand He fed me an intimate revelation that because Josiah and I are both part of the body of Christ, we are eternally connected. Josiah is just on one side of the veil, and I am on the other. The Lord in His brilliance knew I would get this truth. He even gave me a holy visual to connect the dots. My son wasn't cut off from the body of Christ when he entered Heaven. No! That would be a lie! He is on Heaven's side, and I am on earth's side, but nonetheless, we are both alive and moving forward for the Kingdom.

> For as we have many members in one body, but all the members do not have the same function, so we, being many, are one body in Christ, and individually members of one another. (Rom. 12:4–5)

> For in fact the body is not one member but many.
> If the foot should say, "Because I am not a hand, I am not of the body," is it therefore not of the body? And if the ear should say, "Because I am not an eye, I am not of the body," is it therefore not of the body? If the whole body were an eye, where would be the hearing? If the whole were hearing, where would be the smelling? But now God has set the members, each one of them, in the body just as He pleased. (1 Cor. 12:14–18)

This truth touched a chasm in my heart where fear had told me my child was cut off from me—that I was no longer a part of his life. I applied God's Word to my wound, and it brought a calm that took away some of the sting. In His majesty, the Great Physician has seen to my very gradual healing. Mind you, the scar will always remain for this mom. I will never be complete and fully recovered until I enter Heaven's gates, but to the degree God is able here on earth, He will make us well. He is the cure.

This new normal is so very sad, and we all miss Josiah more than words can say, but I will make much of what God has shown me and pass it on to whoever will listen. Applying the truth of the "one body of Christ" gave me the ability to breathe during those first days. I realized that because of our mutual affection for Jesus, Josiah and I were in fact connected and held together within the one body, and this began my healing from the wound of grief and separation.

What a creative, compassionate God we serve. He, in His infinite wisdom, goes so far out of the way to create hidden manna—bits of truth along our paths—to cover and comfort us until we meet our loved ones again. The truth that God planted in my heart about Siah and me being members of one body was such revelation and has nourished and compelled me to keep moving forward in hope.

As I continued reasoning with the Lord concerning the body of Christ, He pointed out even more mind-boggling truth. It was so obvious, but I had never seen it before, nor had I needed it so desperately. You see, in my mind—and I fear in the minds of many within the church—I had thought of the body of Christ as somehow having two parts. Perhaps it is simply because we in the church emphasize the people living on this side far more than those on Heaven's side. We forget that this pale earth is not the end for those in Christ. May I shout this out? Death is of no consequence to those found in Christ! First Corinthians 15:54 says, "So when this corruptible has put on incorruption, and this mortal has put on immortality, then shall be brought to pass the saying that is written: 'Death is swallowed up in victory.'"

Once a person has flown into eternity, we seldom consider what his or her part might be on the other side. The Enemy has worked overtime to diminish the eternal hope God has given us. Since I am a visual learner, the Holy Spirit gave me a picture to bring clarity. This picture is of the person of Jesus Christ in bodily form with a line drawn right down the center—one body with half on earth and the other half in Heaven. This visual emphasized to me that there is only one Lord, one church, and one body—divided by the veil. Isn't that incredible?

> When a brother, sister, or child in Christ leaves this earth, we are still connected because we are part of the same body of Christ.

Ephesians 4:3–6 instructs us to endeavor "to keep the unity of the Spirit in the bond of peace. There is one body and one Spirit, just as you were called in one hope of your calling; one Lord, one faith, one baptism; one God and Father of all, who is above all, and through all, and in you all." In truth, we can conclude and embrace this great comfort. When a brother, sister, or child in Christ leaves this earth, we are still connected because we are part of the same body of Christ.

For this mom, these words of great hope gave me peace and breath in my very being. It was life-giving to know the great length Jesus went to, to defeat death, hell, and the grave and then beyond that to assure me that to some holy degree, Josiah and I are still intact. Difficult as it was and continues to be, I can rest in the eternal truth that although separated for a time, we are both still working for the Kingdom that cannot be shaken.

What if I had walked past this precious piece of truth left on my path? What if I had not recognized the voice of the Holy Spirit or dismissed it in bitterness or anger? Dear one, do not ignore the only One who can truly bring hope. Had I not stopped to investigate this phrase, I might have remained in this spot for far too long—stuck in my grief, ignoring His divine prompts that were attempting to lead me down this unfamiliar path. To not embrace this truth would have been like slamming the door opened by Jesus, which has led me to continual comfort.

The Lord is "the Father of mercies and God of all comfort" (2 Cor. 1:3). "All comfort" in the Greek means every form of solace,[1] but our sources should line up with His Word. We do not need, nor do we want, counterfeit comfort. The counterfeit lasts for an emotional moment, but God's truth lasts for eternity and heals to the core. Understand that "all" comfort is more creative and much larger than our brains can fathom. God goes beyond our earthly thoughts and appears at the most unpredictable moments, bringing His lavish comfort.

Oh, Father, open our eyes and ears to You. We cannot bear to miss one moment of Heaven pressing in.

Josiah, my son, is still connected to my life because and only because my life and his are both found in Christ. Siah is serving God on one side of the veil, and I am serving on the other. We are not cut off from each other, just as Christ would not cut off His very arm. The body of Christ is in fact one.

Pausing to Remember

In the early days of Josiah moving to Heaven, God continued to reveal so much to me in my deep grief. Though the exact chronology of what I'm about to share is lost on me, the Holy Spirit taught me more and more about the church and His body both here on earth and in Heaven.

Communion had always been part of my faith, but it became even more precious in my husband's and my worship experience—not only at church but regularly in our home. Our practice of taking Communion at home began when our friend Ed quietly left a bottle of wine and some matzo (unleavened bread) at our house just days after Josiah's leaving. I recall seeing it on the counter for a few days before realizing the Lord was beckoning me to remember. Luke 22:19 says Jesus "took bread, gave thanks and broke it, and gave it to [the disciples], saying, 'This is My body which is given for you; do this in remembrance of Me.'"

For countless days, whether with my husband or by myself, I would take Communion and remember Jesus. There was a sense of hidden things in this Communion that I could not grasp, and yet I knew I needed to make the effort to be obedient and simply come to the table and recall His body given and blood shed for the forgiveness of my sins. Then one Sunday at church, as I partook in Communion with my dear friend Donna, whose husband, Greg, had recently left this earth, the Lord gave me a picture. Grief was heavy on us both as we were praying together and remembering our families in Heaven.

As we prayed, the Lord interrupted my thoughts with the clear image of a heart in a million pieces; but in one moment, all those pieces, large and small, were put back into their perfect places. The Lord then said, "I am going to put all things back together again!" It astonished me! When He so clearly says something unexpected, whether simple or complex, it has the power to change our very being. My friend Jackie says it best: "When the Lord speaks, it is a seed that literally takes root inside and absolutely changes our very DNA!" We become different in one miraculous moment. With His word, He formed the world. With His word, He can change our hearts. In a moment, He replaced my anguish with hope, beauty from ashes.

To the extent of the faith I was given, I have always believed He would put my heart back together, but this was different. He was driving home that all my brokenness would be mended. He is aware of the deepest places, even those seemingly small ones we don't pay attention to. He will set each piece back together—redeemed, new, perfect, and much, much better in His Kingdom.

The most important point God was speaking to Donna and me in that moment was the reassembling of our families. We both needed to hear and see this life-giving message that in His divine sovereignty, He was delivering. He knew Donna and I needed to have a "look into My eyes and listen to Me" moment. If we would just choose to believe—oh, the comfort it would bring.

Revelation 21:5–6 says,

> Then He who sat on the throne said, "Behold, I make all things new." And He said to me, "Write, for these words are true and faithful."
>
> And He said to me, "It is done! I am the Alpha and the Omega, the Beginning and the End. I will give of the fountain of the water of life freely to him who thirsts."

There is a day coming when we will behold with our own eyes all things made new. When Jesus said "all things," this is exactly what He meant—body, mind, soul, spirit, air, trees, friendships, memories, homes, and family.

Over time, the Lord continued to lead me into extraordinary revelation about Communion and the body of Christ. You may have already seen this, but apart from deep valleys of desperation for Him, I may never have searched for the deeper meaning of His broken body for us. Jesus instituted the Lord's Table, or Communion, right before He was betrayed and crucified. Luke 22:14–20 records the account:

> When the hour had come, He sat down, and the twelve apostles with Him. Then He said to them, "With fervent desire I have desired to eat this Passover with you before I suffer; for I say to you,

I will no longer eat of it until it is fulfilled in the
kingdom of God."

Then He took the cup, and gave thanks, and
said, "Take this and divide it among yourselves; for
I say to you, I will not drink of the fruit of the vine
until the kingdom of God comes."

And He took bread, gave thanks and broke
it, and gave it to them, saying, "This is My body
which is given for you; do this in remembrance
of Me."

Likewise He also took the cup after supper,
saying, "This cup is the new covenant in My blood,
which is shed for you."

Jesus longed for this moment with His friends. This intimate
occasion paints a picture for the body of Christ to follow not only
for generations here on earth but also for eternity. Jesus specified
that He will again drink of the fruit of the vine when the Kingdom
of God comes. I can hear Him saying, "Remember, remember,
remember!"

When the Lord gave me that picture of the heart being put
back together again during Communion, I began associating the
vision with the Communion bread, His broken body. I sensed
Him saying that His body, the bread, would be put back together
again, just like our broken hearts. Knowing that Jesus' physical
body is already healed and He is whole and perfect, I felt as if He
was speaking to me about "us"—the church, the body of Christ.
This led me into an in-depth study of Scripture that refers to bread

being broken and how these verses may foreshadow our lives being broken and given as a testament to the world.

Nothing Is Lost

The Gospels have two accounts of Jesus feeding the masses miraculously via a few loaves of bread and a couple of fish. You probably have read the story many times. But what you may not have noticed is what happened *after* the miracle—after all the people were full. In both accounts, Jesus asked the disciples to gather the fragments of bread that were left over. Yet only in John's account do we read *why* Jesus asked them to do this task. John 6:4–15 says:

> Now the Passover, a feast of the Jews, was near. Then Jesus lifted up His eyes, and seeing a great multitude coming toward Him, He said to Philip, "Where shall we buy bread, that these may eat?" But this He said to test him, for He Himself knew what He would do.
>
> Philip answered Him, "Two hundred denarii worth of bread is not sufficient for them, that every one of them may have a little."
>
> One of His disciples, Andrew, Simon Peter's brother, said to Him, "There is a lad here who has five barley loaves and two small fish, but what are they among so many?"
>
> Then Jesus said, "Make the people sit down." Now there was much grass in the place. So the men sat down, in number about five thousand. And Jesus

took the loaves, and when He had given thanks He distributed them to the disciples, and the disciples to those sitting down; and likewise of the fish, as much as they wanted. So when they were filled, He said to His disciples, "Gather up the fragments that remain, so that nothing is lost." Therefore they gathered them up, and filled twelve baskets with the fragments of the five barley loaves which were left over by those who had eaten. Then those men, when they had seen the sign that Jesus did, said, "This is truly the Prophet who is to come into the world."

Therefore when Jesus perceived that they were about to come and take Him by force to make Him king, He departed again to the mountain by Himself alone.

Did you notice that odd detail? There was nothing whole left—Christ only mentions the fragments. I wonder what those gathering the leftovers were thinking … *Why in the world would our Teacher ask us to gather crumbs of bread?* The trite little pieces must have seemed worthless and, honestly, a hassle to gather. Maybe the larger pieces were of more value and had the potential of providing another meal for tomorrow. But the truth is, day-old bread in biblical times was impossible to eat, as it would be hard as a rock. The disciples would have considered the fragments useless. But the question remains, why gather the fragments? Because fragments are important to Jesus! He said in verse 12, "Gather up the fragments that remain, so that nothing is lost."

His assignment for the disciples was that all leftover pieces be gathered. Friend, He has an assignment for the gathering of your fragments. The Lord Himself has designated that your broken heart be gathered. There may be friends assigned to this task, or perhaps angelic hosts, but the point remains that there is work being done around you. Can you see it? Are you allowing the pieces to be gathered? Or have you perhaps clung so tightly to grief and brokenness that you have unknowingly resisted releasing your pieces into His care?

Nothing is lost. There is not one broken or torn thing that is lost on Christ. He sees, He knows, and in the case of grief and heartbreak, not one bit of our pain is lost on Him. He does nothing in vain, and nothing is worthless to Him. He wants to gather the broken bits, every single fragmented piece. He will keep them until that final day when He makes all things right and sets all things together once again in our hearts and lives. Paul says it this way: "For this reason I also suffer these things; nevertheless I am not ashamed, for I know whom I have believed and am persuaded that He is able to keep what I have committed to Him until that Day" (2 Tim. 1:12).

Fear not! Your pieces are more important to your heavenly Father than you can possibly fathom. Your son, daughter, spouse, or other loved one who has left for the Kingdom is never "lost" or forgotten. Let go of that crippling fear. Jesus has specifically appointed that all these things that concern us—every shattered piece—should be gathered and put into His safe place until that final day.

To drive the point home that much more, let's look at the original Greek text of John 6:12. When Jesus says, "That nothing be lost" (ASV), He is saying just that: *nothing*.

There are so many pieces to grieving a child—so much shattered in one moment. The most troubling in the immediate is not knowing how to move forward. All plans have been destroyed. Our mental lists are torn and scattered. Will we forget? Will my son know my heart is still concerned about his day, although he is now living it out in eternity? We are mothers. It is still our job to keep track of our children and tend to their needs. Our arms feel empty not helping to carry their burdens and not physically holding them.

Look into your basket of fragments. Not one "crumb" of your child has been lost or forgotten—not even the tiniest of morsels—because as Jesus Himself said, "Gather up the fragments ... so that nothing is lost." Bring your basket; look in it with tears, but tears of great hope. Your Master and Creator has a glorious result coming. He even remembers pieces that you have forgotten. He is the "Great Rememberer"! Allow everything to be placed in God's protection, for on "that day," the pieces will once again be made whole and will be restored.

The images in these verses also show us what He is doing spiritually, as if to say, "The fragments of your heart, though torn, are of great value." If you're thinking in the hidden place of your heart, *Oh, not my pieces. Mine aren't important enough,* or *There are too many to gather,* may I ask if you could please, even in your great anguish, choose to believe the Word? Jesus is going out of His way, or rather, this *is* His way, to send His message of hope to you. He is keeping every crumb in what I imagine is a beautiful basket, labeled with your specific name.

Doesn't it bring peace to know all your greatest concerns are being kept safe? All you must do is open your clenched fists and drop the pieces into God's basket of fragments. This contrasts with the Devil's lie that all is lost and floating out in dark space, never to be heard from again. Lies, all lies, that would cause us to not trust our eternal God, who has dominion over all things. He commands the universe. If you have not heard Natalie Grant's song "King of the World," download it, listen on repeat, and let its words encourage you.

The Broken Bread

You may be asking, *Why bread? Why would God use this symbol to speak about reunification and healing?* In the Word, the Lord establishes that the bread of Communion represents His body, which was broken for us. He was showing us something that night before He bore the cross for our sins. He wanted us to remember the sacrifice He made for all humankind. But was He also alluding to a mystery that would be revealed after the Holy Spirit was given? I can imagine myself going back to that very setting as an observer, hearing and thinking, *Wait! I know this Jesus and have watched and listened to Him for three years now. There is always more to what He is saying. There is something familiar about this breaking of the bread and remembering … the miracle of the loaves, the basket of fragments. Is there even more to this Last Supper with Jesus than meets the eye?*

Throughout the New Testament, we find many references to the church being the body of Christ; it's also referred to as bread. I absolutely believe that when Jesus said at the Last Supper, "This is My body, which is broken for you" (1 Cor. 11:24), He was speaking in the immediate about His own flesh. But have you ever wondered if there was something else hidden within His words? In that moment, was Jesus speaking prophetically about us, the church? When Paul later referred to us, the body of Christ, as "bread," this came through revelation—a "this is that" moment for Paul. Examine these passages:

> I speak as to wise men; judge for yourselves what I say. The cup of blessing which we bless, is it not the communion of the blood of Christ? The bread which we break, is it not the communion of the body of Christ? For we, though many, are one bread and one body; for we all partake of that one bread. (1 Cor. 10:15–17)

> I beseech you therefore, brethren, by the mercies of God, that you present your bodies a living sacrifice, holy, acceptable to God, which is your reasonable service. (Rom. 12:1)

> Yet indeed I also count all things loss for the excellence of the knowledge of Christ Jesus my Lord, for whom I have suffered the loss of all things, and count them as rubbish, that I may gain Christ and be found in Him, not having my own righteousness, which is from the law, but that which is through faith in Christ, the righteousness which is from God by faith; that I may know Him and the power of His resurrection, and the fellowship of His sufferings, being conformed to His death, if, by any means, I may attain to the resurrection from the dead. (Phil. 3:8–11)

> Now you are the body of Christ, and members
> individually. (1 Cor. 12:27)

Jesus was broken for us, and now we are broken through the fellowship of His sufferings, as we are His body. When I take the cup and the bread, I remember King Jesus first and foremost, but then I remember that I am also to die to self and be broken and distributed to the world, just as our Jesus set the example.

Our lives as believers are given for a lost world, unbelievers who are watching our next move. They wonder, *What will the follower of Christ do when tragedy comes?* We display strength to others by fully trusting in our God. In the end, our lives as the body on display—pulled apart and given to those who are lost—will be reassembled. Every piece will be back in its perfect place on that day! This was a mystery I'd never noted before. Maybe it's just me, but I needed to further appreciate my broken place in this world and the impact my shattered heart could have on those watching. To know Him and the power of His resurrection and the fellowship of His suffering.

The God of "Together"

Then finally, dear ones, here are a couple of passages that speak to us being gathered together again.

> For the Lord Himself will descend from heaven
> with a shout, with the voice of an archangel, and
> with the trumpet of God. And the dead in Christ
> will rise first. Then we who are alive and remain
> shall be caught up *together* with them in the clouds

> to meet the Lord in the air. And thus, we shall
> always be with the Lord. Therefore comfort one
> another with these words. (1 Thess. 4:16–18)

> For God did not appoint us to wrath, but to obtain
> salvation through our Lord Jesus Christ, who died
> for us, that whether we wake or sleep, we should
> live *together* with Him.
>
> Therefore comfort each other and edify one
> another, just as you also are doing. (1 Thess. 5:9–11)

The word *together* has never meant so much to me! I love 1 Thessalonians 4:18 for the specific way it tells us to comfort one another with these words. This verse brings life to my very bones when I'm down and out. It not only soothes me, but anytime I share it, I can actually see an aha moment—a look of joy or a tear of hope—on the face of the one hearing it. If the Word says to share this truth to bring comfort, then you can trust it will do just that. Tell those who are grieving that we will all live together again. We *will* do life together again!

I also appreciate the order of events we see in these verses. The dead in Christ shall rise first, and *then* those who remain shall be caught up together. This is all a mystery, so bear with me. Your child is already in the presence of God (see 2 Cor. 5:8–10) and living her life with an incredible new body, a spirit body. It can be identified, and it looks just like your child, but even better. Then one day, she and the rest of the dead in Christ will rise, each with an even more incredible body, a glorified body (see 1 Cor. 15:50–52). These bodies will be like the one Christ has in the heavenlies now (see 1 John 3:2). Remember after the resurrection how Jesus walked the earth for forty days, appearing to many (see Acts 1:3)? Well, I am not the sharpest knife in the drawer, but it seems to me that when our loved ones in Christ rise, the world is going to be rocked by what they see with their own eyes. Think of the conversions! (And by the way, I love that my boy will be physically seen on the earth again before the rapture.) Then those who remain here on the earth and have not yet fallen asleep will experience the rapture and be caught up "together" with them in the sky, with those we have loved. God is in every detail, and He is about fulfilling His Word.

Wouldn't we agree that first we'd want to be gathered with our kids? Let's be honest. Ten years into this journey, I finally confessed aloud what has been in my heart for years: "Jesus, you know I love You and trust You with all my heart. You also know the depths of my soul and are aware of my every thought, so I may as well confess with my own lips what You already know. When I get there, I want to see Siah's face first!"

The Holy Spirit responded immediately with an answer I never expected: "Sarah, that's because you don't miss Me. You know I am always with you. But because Josiah is not, that's why you long to see him first." There was no guilt in this; only the Spirit's kindness in helping me make sense of the longing within me. I am never alone and always aware that Jesus is with me. How gracious that He would give me full permission to fall on Siah's neck first and allow us time to talk, cry, catch up, and jump up and down for joy. Then quickly, I will run and fall at the feet of my Savior and King to worship and thank Him.

God is holding all things in place until that day when He gathers us together. For now, we are connected in this moment by the Spirit as members in the body of Christ. But in *that* moment, in the twinkling of an eye, we will be gathered together and united with Jesus … *all together.* And y'all, you'll find this mom huddled somewhere with her entire family as we dogpile a certain Josiah David Berger!

> *al-to-geth-er* (adv.)
> > completely, totally, entirely, wholly,
> > fully, thoroughly, utterly, quite,
> > downright, perfectly, undisputedly

Comfort one another with these words!

Reflection

Ask the Lord to make His Word real to you. List the things that knowingly, or perhaps unknowingly, you have handed over to the Enemy of your soul, assuming they're gone forever. Now in Jesus' name, take the pieces of your heart back, and see them given over to your loving Father for His safekeeping until all things are made new again.

Thank You, Father, for Your safekeeping. I trust You with my broken pieces. In Jesus' name.

chapter 4

hidden manna

We briefly touched on the "hidden manna" the Lord has for us, and I want to dive a little deeper into a few concepts before we go further. It will be helpful for you to understand the terms I use and why I'm open to the ways the Lord has spoken to me and brought me comfort about Josiah being alive in Heaven.

God has guided me into many sweet family memories, not into revisiting the tragic. When considering anything that would ultimately bring me back to a place of tragedy, He has held His hand up to my heart and said, "No."

The Evil One would love nothing more than for you to dwell on the tragic circumstances that led to your child leaving for Home. But the Word says, "Submit to God. Resist the devil and he will flee from you" (James 4:7). Submit to God by thinking on things above! Resist the Devil by not entertaining things below. You will have to choose to think on things above, or else I fear you may never walk forward in hope. "Work the Word," as a friend of mine would always say.

I found myself needing to apply this because when Josiah first left for Heaven, people would say, "I am so sorry Josiah died," or otherwise reference that he was dead. We knew it didn't seem right—something was awry. Because culture has invaded the church, followers of Jesus use terms not ordained by God. We all make more of death than life when Jesus went to the cross to defeat it. I found believers everywhere seem to be wrongly using the term *death* over those who are actually sleeping in Christ.

First Corinthians 2:6–11 speaks to this holy insight the Father gave me:

> However, we speak wisdom among those who are mature, yet not the wisdom of this age, nor of the rulers of this age, who are coming to nothing. But we speak the wisdom of God in a mystery, the hidden wisdom which God ordained before the ages for our glory, which none of the rulers of this age knew; for had they known, they would not have crucified the Lord of glory.
>
> But as it is written:
>
> "Eye has not seen, nor ear heard,
> Nor have entered into the heart of man
> The things which God has prepared for those
> who love Him."
>
> But God has revealed them to us through His Spirit. For the Spirit searches all things, yes, the deep things of God. For what man knows the

things of a man except the spirit of the man which
is in him?

Friend, God has given us permission to go deep into Scripture if we dare. He has given us the mind of Christ—brilliant minds He can entrust with brilliant truth concerning eternity. The Spirit living in us longs to show us more!

The first seemingly obvious, biblically founded word of hope was this powerful truth, "Josiah is alive!" This may not seem like a "deep" thing of God—so obvious, so clear, right? However, sometimes the most obvious and powerful points are the ones the Enemy dulls the church to and attempts to keep hidden from them—especially those who grieve. If you are grieving a child who has left for Heaven, may I with a broken heart beg you—please, stop making your son's or daughter's story about death. Please, take your thoughts captive (see 2 Cor. 10:5). For the saint of God, the story is never about death but eternal life!

Our family has always referred to Josiah as being alive. Never, ever have we used the *d* word over our son. I believe the Bible proves this is not a term that even Christ preferred! In the story of Lazarus in John 11, Jesus says in verse 4, "This sickness is not unto death." In his own words, Jesus is saying Lazarus's sickness, his story, is not "about, directed toward, or pertaining to" death,[1] but for the glory of God that the Son of God might be exalted. Think about this. Jesus is saying that Lazarus's story is not only *not* about death but is entirely about life and Jesus' power over death.

A few verses later we can peer even deeper into the heart of Christ concerning even speaking the *d* word. John 11:11–15 (Did you catch that 11:11?) says:

> These things He said, and after that He said to them, "Our friend Lazarus sleeps, but I go that I may wake him up."
>
> Then His disciples said, "Lord, if he sleeps, he will get well." However, Jesus spoke of his death, but they thought that He was speaking about taking rest in sleep.
>
> Then Jesus said to them plainly, "Lazarus is dead. And I am glad for your sakes that I was not there, that you may believe. Nevertheless, let us go to him."

The disciples were asking, "Do we really need to go see him?" Earlier they were concerned about the dangers in the area because some wanted to stone Jesus. When Jesus spoke of Lazarus's physical death, they thought He was talking about slumber. So Jesus had to tell them bluntly that Lazarus was dead.

Jesus preferred using the term *sleep*. He knew Lazarus was not actually dead but was only sleeping on this side of the veil. He was alive on the other side, in paradise. But because the others didn't understand, He had to use straightforward language: *dead*. It probably pained Jesus to use this term about his friend. It certainly was not His first choice in words. Jesus was speaking God. A foreign language, but a language we as eternal beings need to study and learn.[2]

When ministering to those who are mourning loved ones in Christ, remember to use terms that acknowledge truth. Speaking words pertaining to life and not death will literally change the countenances of those who grieve. We quickly came to discover that the term *alive in Heaven* concerning Josiah is similar to the term *asleep*. The phrase is life-giving to those who have loved ones living in Heaven. Don't use past-tense terms, referring to a loved one alive in Heaven as a *was*. "Oh, he *was* such a good friend. He *was* a wonderful dad." Heaven has not stopped your dad from being wonderful, right? His legacy continues even though he now lives in eternity. A believer living in Heaven is *still* your friend, *still* a part of your family!

> Speaking words pertaining to life and not death will literally change the countenances of those who grieve.

Jesus said to Martha in John 11:25–26, "I am the resurrection and the life. He who believes in Me, though he may die, he shall live. And whoever lives and believes in Me shall never die. Do you believe this?" If we in fact believe this, it will be natural to stop using the terms *dead* or *death* or *was* over those who are certainly alive in Christ!

Don't think I'm living in denial. I live in the anguish of the reality of it all. I also know, because of the Spirit's leading, that my son—just like Lazarus—is only sleeping to us and radically alive on the other side of a very thin veil. Josiah's story is not about death— rather, it is all about Jesus defeating death and bestowing the power of life eternal. Josiah is alive!

John 11:44 says, "He who had died came out bound hand and foot with graveclothes, and his face was wrapped with a cloth. Jesus said to them, 'Loose him, and let him go.'" We likewise need to remove the graveclothes that we imagine bind our loved ones, and set them free. Josiah is not bound up in tattered sheets in some scary, dark place but is alive and wearing what I imagine is a happy, sunny-colored T-shirt and shorts! Alive, alive, alive!

A Cloud of Witnesses

Another topic that has been misunderstood by culture, and by some within the church, is speaking aloud to the Heavens.

In those initial days, weeks, months, if you need to verbalize to a heavenly audience, then do so. Counselors encourage those in the throes of grief to verbalize their emotions. The separation from our loved one is an assault on our very being and on the Lord's original plan for humankind. He created us to live forever, and when forever is cut off and the devastation of this temporary separation is unbearable, talk! It is emotionally crippling to be told either by culture or a well-meaning friend that your loved one in Heaven will never hear your words.

The painful truth is that until we are reunited, our words will not receive a verbal response. Our confidence and trust must lie in the goodness of Christ. How often the Lord allows our loved ones to hear through the veil, I am not certain; however, I *am* certain that if it is necessary and edifying, He'll relay our words somehow. He does not withhold any good thing (see Ps. 84:11). What harm in believing the Word? What comfort in the possibility?

Hebrews 11 is a riveting account of all who have believed in Messiah and have gone before us into Glory, eternity. Then we come to the following verses in Hebrews 12, which serve to heighten our awareness that we are being witnessed by brothers and sisters, angels and saints, and ultimately—and most importantly—by the Lord Himself.

> Therefore we also, since we are surrounded by so great a cloud of witnesses, let us lay aside every weight, and the sin which so easily ensnares us, and let us run with endurance the race that is set before us, looking unto Jesus, the author and finisher of our faith, who for the joy that was set before Him endured the cross, despising the shame, and has sat down at the right hand of the throne of God. (vv. 1–2)

Hebrews 12:1 brings comfort and also spurs us on to good works. How wonderful is the idea of our loved ones looking in and how right God is in knowing that we would need a heavenly accountability until the day we ourselves arrive in the Kingdom. To reject this truth is to deny the very Word of God.

The Lord is so smart to follow up with verse 2, speaking of looking to Jesus, who is the Alpha and Omega of our faith. He knows we who grieve are vulnerable, so the Lord is going to make sure we have the right perspective and balance. In Berger paraphrase, I put it like this: "What a blessing to be linked to the church in Heaven through accountability, *but* the most important thing to keep in front of us is Jesus. Don't focus so much on the cloud that you lose sight of the King."

It couldn't be clearer: We are being watched by a glorious host. The cloud of witnesses, the hosts of Heaven, are cheering us on, and I think they are thrilled when they see a follower of Christ who truly believes and is living in the reality that they are alive, active, and aware.

I was born again in 1975, during my sophomore year of high school. Although I don't recall ever feeling alone in my childhood and I grew up in a loving home with some of the most faithful friends, something stood out profoundly to me after saying yes to Jesus. I remember the next day walking the halls of Walnut High with a keen sense that I was not alone. I had this internal knowing that God was with me, and I let Him know. I talked out loud to Him, and I talked with Him in my heart.

All these years later, the glory of knowing I am never alone still stands out to me. Whether I feel it or not, there is a deep knowing that *Jesus*, my Savior, is always there. He is watching me, and I am accountable to Him for all my actions. He flat-out goes with me into every environment, hostile or otherwise; He is with me!

God's eyes upon me and His presence with me should be enough, but having a child in Heaven takes it to another level.

Just as I want my Father to be pleased with my life, I also want my friends and family in Heaven to be also. Hebrews 12:1–2 clearly indicates that there is a beautiful accountability in which the Father intended for us to walk. The King James Version of the Bible uses the term "compassed about" to describe our relationship to that great cloud of witnesses who are looking on. The definition from Strong's Concordance of the original Greek word shows the beauty and full meaning of these verses. *Surrounded* in verse 1 literally means "to lie all around, i.e. inclose, encircle, hamper ... be bound (compassed) with, hang about."[3] How kind of God to provide this great comfort. He knew before the creation of the world that our human hearts would find strength in understanding that we're surrounded by a heavenly host.

Unfortunately, the church has lost much of this comfort. Jesus intended for those of us left here to take great hope in the truth that our beloved in Christ who have gone on before us are active in the Kingdom and that they are aware of circumstances on earth. Instead, we listen to naysayers, even Christians, who embrace a lie, taking some sort of warped joy from denying the truth of the Word and glorifying death instead. Why?

I remember years ago, my husband shared at a believer's memorial service, where he made much of Heaven and how alive this saint of Christ was right then. Afterward, a critical woman approached him, her countenance lacking all joy as she scolded him for his disrespect to the family when making much of the departed saint being alive. She would have far preferred we use words like *death* and *loss* for the entire service. But our approach was worth it: the family was filled with great hope and left so encouraged. The reminder of their loved one being alive brought much strength and eased their heartbreak.

The woman who went away choosing to clutch death close to her heart possessed a strange attitude that lives in many believers. They somehow relish embracing the very thing that Jesus came to destroy—death! This brings to mind the many people who "went away" from Jesus because they were offended by the truth that would heal their very souls.

> When they heard this, they were amazed. So they left him and *went away*. (Matt. 22:22 NIV)

> "And I was afraid, so I *went away* and hid your talent in the ground. See, you still have what is yours." (Matt. 25:25 NASB)

> But he was deeply dismayed by these words, and he *went away* grieving; for he was one who owned much property. (Mark 10:22 NASB)

When Josiah left for Heaven, Steve and I dove into the Word to discover every nuance we could about his new life there. We are eternally thankful that we concluded just the opposite of the naysayers. Clearly, Scripture teaches it is *we* here on earth who are in the land of the dying. Saints who have gone on are in the land of the *living*, "swallowed up by life" (2 Cor. 5:4) and more alive than any of us here on earth will ever be!

Let's not overlook an important little phrase in Hebrews 12:2 that speaks of Jesus, "who for the joy that was set before Him." What is that joy? Eternal life! This is the primary reason Jesus endured the cross. Death is defeated, and now our King sits at the right hand of the throne of God. Fellow believer, it's time to embrace truth. It's time to receive hope!

Randy Alcorn explains:

> Because of pervasive distortions of what heaven is like, it's common for Christians not to look forward to heaven—or even to dread it. I think there's only one explanation for how these appalling viewpoints have gripped so many of God's people: Satan. Demonic deception.
>
> Jesus said of the devil, "When he lies, he speaks his native language, for he is a liar and the father of lies" (John 8:44). Some of Satan's favorite lies are about heaven. Revelation 13:6 tells us the satanic beast "opened his mouth to blaspheme God, and to slander his name and his dwelling place and those who live in heaven." Our enemy slanders three things: God's person, God's people, and God's place—heaven.[4]

God Nods

Any and every time I have had a heavenly experience, it has always and only been a spontaneous and unexpected pure work of God! I have never sought after a soulish connection with Josiah, and the Lord has never allowed me to even conceive in my heart or mind the way He might minister to me concerning Josiah (or anything else, for that matter). When in fact He coordinates what our family calls a "God Nod," it's mind-boggling, magnificent, and sometimes just fun. God Nods are special, supernatural moments that radically contribute to the healing process and come when we least expect them. At times, Jesus seems to go after tending wounded places in our hearts, while other times He just wants to bring a smile to our faces.

When the Pharisees and Sadducees asked Jesus for a sign, He called a spade a spade: "'A wicked and adulterous generation seeks after a sign, and no sign shall be given to it except the sign of the prophet Jonah.' And He left them and departed" (Matt. 16:4). In my own words, friends: do *not* seek for signs or, in our language, God Nods. If and when the Lord meets you with a God Nod, it is a sheer gift of grace. Signs are something to believe in but not to believe *for*. If you are trying to muster up a dream, a word, or—careful now—a visitation, then I think it almost certain you will create something false. *But* when He does give a sign, there is no second-guessing, and He alone receives all the credit.

I've spoken these words to the Lord many a time: "Father, I believe in You and will follow You forever. I don't need a sign to convince me of Your love for me. I don't need a sign for me to believe. I believe forever. But because You're a good God and You give good gifts to Your children, if ever You do bring a sign, it's merely divine sugar on top because You like giving to those who believe." Check all things against the Word, His Spirit, and His nature.

Leviticus 19:31 says, "Give no regard to mediums and familiar spirits; do not seek after them, to be defiled by them: I am the LORD your God." Chapter 20 continues: "And the person who turns to mediums and familiar spirits, to prostitute himself with them, I will set My face against that person and cut him off from his people. Consecrate yourselves therefore, and be holy, for I am the LORD your God" (vv. 6–7).

King Saul crossed that line, and his life was never the same. We see in 1 Samuel 28 that he consulted a medium and participated in what is forbidden by God—a séance. The same day he consulted the medium, he and his sons were killed. Do not ever cross this line, or you are opening yourself up to demonic activity.

If you have crossed this line by seeking a medium or if you have read books that endorse unchristian practices, I recommend that you approach a pastor or the elders of a solid Christian church and request counseling. There is an absolute need for repentance. I realize some may have previously been ignorant that this activity is forbidden by God. I encourage you to find a biblically sound church that stands fast to the entire canon of Scripture.

> Who has put wisdom in the mind?
> Or who has given understanding to the heart?
> (Job 38:36)

> For as the heavens are higher than the earth,
> So are My ways higher than your ways,
> And My thoughts than your thoughts. (Isa. 55:9)

Inspired Dreams

What about dreams? Is it possible for a saint to show up in a dream? Is that biblically sound? This whole concept may be something you're not familiar with, so I want to pause here to look at one of many examples in the Word of God in which He used dreams to give instruction, protection, warning, and wisdom.

In the book of Daniel, Nebuchadnezzar, the king of Babylon, on more than one occasion experienced what I call a "God dream." One dream in particular horrified the king, as it was a prophetic warning about what his future would look like if he didn't repent. Upon interpreting the dream, Daniel gave this advice to the king: "O king, let my advice be acceptable to you; break off your sins by being righteous, and your iniquities by showing mercy to the poor. Perhaps there may be a lengthening of your prosperity" (Dan. 4:27).

I bring up this dream to reference one of the many times the Lord spoke via a dream in the Word—but also to draw attention to a bystander within the dream. We gaze right past him, yet we know all things are written very intentionally by God's hand. So who is this character? Nebuchadnezzar references him in Daniel 4:13: "I saw in the visions of my head while on my bed, and there was a watcher, a holy one, coming down from heaven."

Later in the same chapter, Daniel references him again but with more detail:

> And whereas the king saw a watcher and a holy one
> coming down from heaven, and saying, Hew down
> the tree, and destroy it; nevertheless leave the stump

> of the roots thereof in the earth, even with a band of
> iron and brass, in the tender grass of the field, and let
> it be wet with the dew of heaven: and let his portion
> be with the beasts of the field, till seven times pass
> over him; this is the interpretation, O king, and it is
> the decree of the Most High, which is come upon
> my lord the king. (vv. 23–24 ASV)

Bible scholars are not in complete agreement as to whether there was one messenger from Heaven or two. I personally believe there were two because of the distinct words used to describe the messengers. If there were indeed two beings that God ordained to participate in Nebuchadnezzar's dream, just who were they? To find the answer, we must look at what these words mean in the original Hebrew language of the Old Testament.

"Watcher" comes from the word `îr, which in the original Hebrew means "angel" (as in, guardian). "Holy one" is taken from the Hebrew word qadîš, which translates "saint."[5]

Why do I mention this? To give biblical reference to the fact that saints are recorded in the Word as showing up in dreams. Notice how in verse 23 Daniel makes it known that the watcher/angel and the holy one/saint were coming down from Heaven and speaking!

Years ago, a friend explained what I was experiencing in my many God dreams. The Lord was presenting riddles and enigmas for me to solve along the way. It was said of the prophet Daniel that he was given the ability to solve enigmas, interpret dreams, and so on (see 5:12). She explained to me that the solving of an enigma means the untying of knots. There is something to be solved, a deeper meaning.

In my own experience, I take most every lucid dream to the Lord. If it is incredibly clear, with vivid detail, I will bring it to the Lord and ask Him if there is something He is trying to say beyond the obvious. I tell Him, "Father God, if this is You, I don't want to miss a thing. But if this is just the pizza that I ate for dinner speaking, I want to forget all about it. I simply do not want to miss a dream, riddle, or enigma You have for me."

Remember Job? God may speak this way and man does not perceive it! So many people have been given dreams via the Lord and too frequently do not even stop to think, *Is that for me?* Missing a divine directive feels suffocating to me. Missing anything God says at all feels like handling something sacred as if common. Stop, look, and listen. (More on this to come!)

Finally, we should ask, What spirit lives within us? Are we offended by God when He shows up in ways we weren't expecting or when He perhaps goes about things in ways or with timing that we just don't like? *How dare He show up like that. Or, I don't believe He would ever do that!* The stories in this book will certainly challenge a religious mind and possibly ruffle the feathers of some. Alas, unless you have known such grief and pain, you possibly have had no need of this matchless grace.

Reflection

> Then he opened his mouth in blasphemy against
> God, to blaspheme His name, His tabernacle, and
> those who dwell in heaven. (Rev. 13:6)

Okay, ladies, it's time for a powerful revelation! The above verse exposes the dark plan of the Enemy, and God wants us to see it. Here we evaluate where we are concerning the Kingdom. If you have been entertaining thoughts that make less of God, less of His name that is above every other name, less of Heaven, and less of those living eternal life, now is your opportunity.

Using the following questions, please take the time to be honest before the Lord. Confess, good or bad.

1. Have you been entertaining lies about the Lord?
2. Have you forgotten the power that is in the name of Jesus?
3. Have you dismissed Heaven as if it were a lower form of earth, rather than the glorious eternal Home for the saint of God?
4. Have you forgotten how the saints in Heaven are more alive than we are here on earth?

I will always point you toward the Word of God and repentance, so here we go. Repentance isn't simply an apology; to *repent* is to think differently, that is, to reconsider.

I can hear John the Baptist's words ringing in my ear. "Repent, for the kingdom of heaven is at hand!" (Matt. 3:2). Reconsider, friend; the Kingdom of God is at hand.

chapter 5

a timely note

The LORD shall preserve you from all evil;
He shall preserve your soul.
The LORD shall preserve your going out and your coming in
From this time forth, and even forevermore.

Psalm 121:7–8

We were approaching the one-year anniversary of Josiah leaving for Heaven, and I was faced with a decision. Did I trust the Lord for more comfort, or did I believe what the world kept throwing at me? The problem was that the Enemy of my very soul kept throwing a specific lie toward me—via the people of God! When well-meaning people recite worldly pablum as if it is God's truth, we must take caution! When worthless counsel is delivered to us who are vulnerable, we must lean even further into Christ for His better way.

Fellow believer, please check all your preconceived ideas with the Word of God before applying them to those who are walking through grief—or anyone, for that matter. I am speaking about both giving counsel and receiving it. If delivering counsel, attend to your words as if from the Lord's very mouth, and do not speak on what you do not know. I've thought back on some awful counsel that I gave before walking this path, and I am horrified that, at times, I may have unintentionally heaped on more grief and sorrow than grace.

Our intent is to deliver the same comfort God has perfectly shown us in our own trials, but we are certainly fallible messengers. Second Corinthians 1:3–5 says:

> Blessed be the God and Father of our Lord Jesus Christ, the Father of mercies and God of all comfort, who comforts us in all our tribulation, that we may be able to comfort those who are in any trouble, with the comfort with which we ourselves are comforted by God. For as the sufferings of Christ abound in us, so our consolation also abounds through Christ.

It was only two weeks before Josiah's birthday and also the one-year anniversary of his Homegoing. I wept bitter, ugly tears as early one morning I drove into downtown Franklin to get a haircut. I knew my stylist well, so I didn't mind looking my worst. Looks are simply low on the priority scale when one is experiencing grief.

As I pulled into a nearly vacant parking lot, I ran into one of my dearest friends and her son. Sweet Kim, who is in Heaven now, had loved on my children well through the years, and her son Elisha is a great friend to our kiddos. Our boys had spent many a day doing what boys do—Huckleberry Finn–type antics, such as climbing trees, shooting guns, riding motorcycles, and so on. We greeted one another with tight hugs, as they knew all too well that Josiah's birthday was approaching.

I shared my current dilemma with them and explained why the floodgate of tears had opened on that particular morning: "Guys, I have been told by several well-meaning people that the second year of grief is worse than the first. I've been pouring out my heart to the Lord, declaring that I do not believe this! I've asked Him for proof of this in His Word, and I cannot see an example of the Lord of all comfort decreeing a second year worse with grief. There are many chapters in the Word I've applied to my wound, but never have I noted that He would heap more pain on my broken heart. I know His nature, and their counsel doesn't match up. What in the world?

"The sort of folk who speak painful untruths you might deem Job's friends. When they kept their mouths shut, they ministered to Job, but when they began to speak, they only brought pain with it. I mean, why would anyone say, 'You are going to hurt worse your second year'!? What a strange, hopeless statement from people who have not experienced this level of grief. Not to be cavalier, but I am not buying it!

"I've wept all the way into town, crying out to the Lord. I told Him that I renounce the lies spoken over me and that I am believing Him for more comfort, more life, more truth about Heaven, and more hearing and understanding of His Word in the Scriptures. I'm praying, *More of You, Lord, to apply to my broken heart. All the worldly counsel or psychology of men—I don't receive it. They seem to say that You are going to show up less. I refuse this, Father. I choose to believe You are going to show up even more in this second year. More of You.*"

God wanted to comfort this mom
with His immensely powerful
assurance that He is concerned
for us here on this poor earth.

My friends and I hugged again as we agreed with the God of hope in that parking lot in August 2010. My tears turned into eternal resolve, and I was better. I was encouraged. I was hope filled again rather than hopeless! I went my way, got a great haircut, and had a sort of bounce back in my step. Only God can do that. I returned to the parking lot, still nearly vacant that Saturday morning. I approached my car, opened the door, and began to slip inside when I noticed a small piece of paper at my feet, precisely placed right near my car door. I thought, *Wait! That might be for me.* I took one step backward, picked the paper up, and slid into the seat.

I would be lying if I said, "And much to my surprise ...," because at this point in my walk, I live more in the "what if" than the "probably not" side of life. In more of an "of course You would" moment, I read my note from God. Printed there on the top of the paper were these words: "Knit together in Love." Beneath them was the Scripture reference "Col. 2:2." I said aloud, "This is for me, Lord!" Another God Nod! "I'll read this verse as soon as I get home." I had no Bible app at that time, as we were still in the flip phone era.

When I walked through my door, I beelined straight to my Bible. Talk about a specific answer to my ask. At the top of this chapter, the heading read, "Not Philosophy, but Christ." Not

pablum, not psychology, not wisdom of man, not philosophy ...
but *Christ*!

> For I want you to know what a great conflict I have
> for you and those in Laodicea, and for as many as
> have not seen my face in the flesh, that their hearts
> may be encouraged, being knit together in love,
> and attaining to all riches of the full assurance of
> understanding, to the knowledge of the mystery of
> God, both of the Father and of Christ, in whom are
> hidden all the treasures of wisdom and knowledge.
> (Col. 2:1–3)

Oh, and there is much more! Verses 4–5 continue,

> Now this I say lest anyone should deceive you with
> persuasive words. For though I am absent in the
> flesh, yet I am with you in spirit, rejoicing to see
> your good order and the steadfastness of your faith
> in Christ.

There you go! Such a distinct word and straight from the mouth
of Paul via the Holy Spirit. God is mind-blowing! Seriously, ladies,
the Word has an answer for every ask; whether it be yea or nay, there
is an answer. God wanted to comfort this mom with His immensely
powerful assurance that He is concerned for us here on this poor
earth. That we are knit together in love and that He has more treasure and mystery for us along the way. Equally, He tells us to be

careful of what we listen to. Don't let them fool you with persuasive words (that is, "The second year is going to be harder!"). No! God is with us.

My note from God remained in my Bible for several years, tucked right there in Colossians 2. Sometime later, a friend noticed my Bible was literally falling apart and asked if he could possibly have it rebound for me as a gift. With much fear and trepidation, I finally agreed and parted with my Word for several weeks to have it physically put back together again. I was sure to search well through the pages for each little special note I had tucked into chapters before sending it off.

While it was still being rebound, I recalled my note and not pulling it out. Upon receiving my beautiful Bible made anew, I went immediately to Colossians to find the note was no longer there. I confess, I was pretty heartbroken, but because I live expectantly, I wouldn't doubt it if in God's holy happenstance, He drops it again along my path. I can't help but imagine that He has a collection of all things tender and dear that were lost here on earth that are found once again in the Kingdom.

P.S. God showed up in power in year two. The pages of this book are evidence that He has never stopped showing up with His comfort, revealing more treasure and mystery along the way. Pick up your mat—let's walk! (See John 5:8 NIV.)

Reflection

Now this I say lest anyone should deceive you with persuasive words. (Col. 2:4)

Have you fallen victim to persuasive words? Have you possibly given yourself over to knowledge that is not found within the pages of Scripture? Have you perhaps felt a red flag at times and didn't realize it was the Holy Spirit warning, "Don't watch; don't read; don't listen"?

List three true terms found in the Word, and describe how they make you feel. Then list three lies and how they affected you. Remember, "you shall know the truth, and the truth shall make you free" (John 8:32).

chapter 6

active duty

But as it is written:
"Eye has not seen, nor ear heard,
Nor have entered into the heart of man
The things which God has prepared for those who love Him."
But God has revealed them to us through His Spirit. For
the Spirit searches all things, yes, the deep things of God.
1 Corinthians 2:9–10

For the gifts and the calling of God are irrevocable.
Romans 11:29

During the fall of 2010, many days passed with the same seemingly arbitrary idea running through my mind: *Josiah is participating in warfare.* As followers of Christ, we know and believe we are all a part of the armies of God, but until now I had never really taken this to heart. I was talking myself out of the possibility when, finally, the thought occurred to me that this may again be the Holy Spirit trying to tell me something.

I searched the Scripture and found several references to the armies of God—verses I'd known for the greater part of my Christian walk but had not been given cause to ponder so deeply.

Second Kings 6:15–17 says:

> And when the servant of the man of God arose early and went out, there was an army, surrounding the city with horses and chariots. And his servant said to him, "Alas, my master! What shall we do?"
>
> So he answered, "Do not fear, for those who are with us are more than those who are with them." And Elisha prayed, and said, "LORD, I pray, open his eyes that he may see." Then the LORD opened the eyes of the young man, and he saw. And behold, the mountain was *full of horses and chariots of fire all around Elisha.*

Revelation 19:14 speaks directly to the "military" of Heaven. It says, "And the armies in heaven, clothed in fine linen, white and clean, followed Him on white horses."

And then there's 2 Timothy 2:3–4:

> You therefore must endure hardship as a good soldier of Jesus Christ. No one engaged in warfare entangles himself with the affairs of this life, that he may please him who enlisted him as a soldier.

Even now I am recalling how at a very young age, Josiah David loved for me to read from his *Beginner's Bible*—particularly the battle stories. His namesake, David, was among his favorites, especially the story of David and Goliath. He had memorized every word. We would take turns as precious little blond Siah would recite a line, and then I'd say one. I would read, "The LORD doesn't save by using a sword or a spear. And everyone who is here will know it." And then: "The battle belongs to the LORD!" Josiah would excitedly say—lisp and all![1]

Josiah still has a warrior spirit, and the Lord was getting ready to present that to me in the most beautiful, creative way through the Word, His still, small voice, and physical signs that were beyond my expectation. The Lord was indeed dropping another crumb onto my path to persuade me to take the next step. Another "Come on. This way. Come, let us reason" moment. So one day, while standing alone in my kitchen, I spoke aloud to the Lord:

"Father, I keep having these thoughts about Siah—that he is somehow involved with some sort of warfare in Heaven. Is that true? Is that from You? You created him to fight, and I remember well that he almost chose to go into the military rather than pursue college. Am I crazy, Lord? You know I only want the truth. I do not want some vain imagination. I don't need to pretend; I just need You! You tell me what is true!"

Immediately in my spirit I heard, "Being confident of this very thing, that He who has begun a good work in you will complete it until the day of Jesus Christ" (Phil. 1:6). I knew at the speed of God exactly what the Lord wanted me to know! It took my very breath away in amazement.

In that moment, I understood Philippians 1:6 in all its full-ness. We always allude to God completing what He began in us on *this* side of the veil. As in, God will complete what He began in your life while you are still here on the earth. Funny how we can recite this entire verse from memory but be blinded to those last few important words, "until the day of Jesus Christ," which refer to a time that is still approaching. Regardless of your personal thoughts as to the "when" of Jesus' return, the point remains, He has not yet. Therefore, God's message to me, to us, is that He is still completing the good work He began in us on the day of our salvation, and that work will continue on both sides of the veil until *the* day of Jesus' return.

> God is still completing what He began in you and me, and that won't stop when we ourselves finish our lives here on earth.

So what the Spirit was saying through His Word was "Yes, what I put in Josiah to accomplish is still being completed until the day I return to establish the Kingdom here on earth." I was astonished! The Holy Spirit continued to drop these amazing truths into my heart as I approached Him. Heaven is more than I could imagine! My son's life never ended but is only and always continuing. Just as it was here on earth, Siah's life is filled with adventure and wonder.

God is still completing what He began in you and me, and that won't stop when we ourselves finish our lives here on earth.

You see, to the believer in Christ Jesus, death is of no consequence. Once we receive Christ as Savior, our lives are forever—eternal. Though our physical bodies may die, we do not! When we breathe our last, we immediately and with no delay step right into eternal life. And there, Jesus continues to complete what He began in us on earth.

So in one word—yes. The answer to my question was and is *yes*! What an unexpected, spontaneous move of the Holy Spirit! When Philippians 1:6 immediately came to my mind, it indeed magnified the Lord Jesus in my heart and brought a wave of eternal, supernatural joy. I felt permission to be excited for my son, knowing he has been given a role and is participating in a heavenly plan.

Does that encourage you? Your child in Christ has not missed out on his or her calling or purpose but rather is living in the fulfillment of that calling in Heaven. The good works God has called your loved one to have not ended; they are being completed, right now, as you read. Until the day of Christ Jesus, God is working His plan in each believer's life, no matter which side of Heaven we're living on. What a glorious promise!

Confirmation from God

The Lord continued to bring a witness and strength to my heart. (Anytime I think I've heard from God, I ask for evidence from Him. I'll remind you time and time again of the need to always keep Jesus and the Word at the forefront. I know well that the Enemy of our souls can twist Scripture to try to confuse and corrupt God's intent.) As I meditated on Philippians 1:6, it was obvious that it made much of Jesus and gave me more clarity into God's intent, but even with that in mind, I began asking for a witness.

First John 4:1–2 says, "Beloved, do not believe every spirit, but test the spirits, whether they are of God; because many false prophets have gone out into the world. By this you know the Spirit of God: Every spirit that confesses that Jesus Christ has come in the flesh is of God."

God is so good to set parameters. He doesn't want any of us to believe a lie, and so I asked, "Father, this sounds like You, but is it You? If so, because You want me safe, please confirm it to me! In Jesus' name and for Your glory."

When Josiah left for Heaven, I begged God at every turn for His instruction on how to walk this heartbreaking road. It was already devastating beyond imagination, yet the thought of stepping out of His will in this process kept me clinging so tightly to His every word. Psalm 119:77 says, "Surround me with your tender mercies so I may live, for your instructions are my delight" (NLT).

In His step-by-step direction for me, one thing I felt sure was better for my soul was to wait to go through any photos. I realize that poring over family photos may be a good thing for some people, if He directs it, but for me He said, "No!" If you're not sure what's right for you, may I gently suggest inquiring of the Lord? It seems to me that it is not in God's nature to heap sorrow upon sorrow, so if looking at photos would send you to the corner, crying until you can't breathe, then wait.

Two days after I received the word about Josiah being a warrior in Heaven, I woke up knowing it was time to look through photos. As God's timing is perfect, photos of our son Cody, who was graduating that year, were due soon for his yearbook. I'd put this off while waiting for the Spirit's lead, but I now sat down on the floor with undeniable anticipation and joy. This only made sense now because it was God wooing me to the task, and I knew the Lord was right there, helping me along the way. So I laughed and I cried, but not with tears of sadness that Siah wasn't with us. Rather, I wept because time was passing so quickly and all four of my babies—Heather, Josiah, Cody, and Destiny—had grown so fast!

Missing Josiah's face and his physical presence was indescribable, but my knowledge that he was continuing to live his life was increasing more and more with every intimate step the Father carried me. My son being very much alive was not only the fulfillment of God's promise in the Word but was becoming even more real through the living Word in me. He was becoming more and more alive to this mom as Jesus revealed more and more of the beauty of eternal life and Heaven. The focus had always been eternity, but it was as if God gave me holy binoculars to allow a deeper look into the Kingdom.

Ongoing Destiny

I passed the entire morning going through photos, finding adorable pics of Cody for the yearbook. Then, out of the blue, I came across two photos I'd seen before but had completely forgotten, of Josiah visiting Fort Campbell during his junior year of high school. This visit to the base came during a season when he seriously considered joining the military.

When he had first mentioned that he was considering enlisting, my eyes had welled up and I held back tears. The idea of war had felt scary and dangerous to me. I hid my face from him so he couldn't see my tears and replied, "Buddy, the most important thing is that you do what you feel the Father is telling you to do!" I never wanted to influence my kids to do my wishes but instead urged them to press into Christ for their answers.

In both photos, he has an army helmet and a military vest (think, helmet of salvation and breastplate of righteousness). It took my breath away as I remembered what the Lord had spoken to me just two days prior. Immediately, I heard the Holy Spirit say, "You put those pictures up where you can see them, and every time you do, you remember that you have a son who serves in the military." Mind you, that word from the Holy Spirit came at the speed of God. I'm not sure if this is how others hear Him, but for me, it seems I couldn't in my human mind even catch up to the words.

Oh, the kindness of the Lord to go *way* beyond what we can ask or imagine to give us what we need in the perfect moment. We don't know what to ask at times and can't even imagine how He might answer, but it is always extravagant! Matthew 6:8 says, "Your Father knows the things you have need of before you ask Him." That our eternal God would plan out our days in such synchronicity as to compel a grieving mom to look through a pile of photos to receive a gift of comfort is something I'll never get over! This is His way.

Oh, but wait! The Lord brought yet another witness to Josiah's ongoing calling and purpose, and to this day it has impacted my life more than any other heavenly experience I've ever had. This event drove home the beauty of the body of Christ as I had never understood before. The Creator of the universe went out of His way to prove to me that the body of Christ does indeed work together on both sides of eternity to accomplish what He wills.

Unexpected Embrace

I do not pray for these alone, but also for those who will believe in Me through their word; that *they all may be one*, as You, Father, are in Me, and I in You; that *they also may be one in Us*, that the world may believe that You sent Me. And the glory which You gave Me I have given them, that *they may be one just as We are one*: I in them, and You in Me; that they *may be made perfect in one*, and that the world may know that You have sent Me, and have loved them as You have loved Me. (John 17:20–23)

A few months later, our family was in a really rough season as we approached the holidays that would mark Josiah's second Christmas away. Our daughter Heather had been in Spain, studying for a semester, and she was now stranded in Europe due to an unusual snowstorm. Our dog Samson, one of Josiah's favorites, was getting ready to leave for Heaven. (Yes, I believe animals go to Heaven. Many Scriptures mention them there.)

We had been on the phone with Heather throughout the day as she called from London, hoping to get on the next flight back home. The airport was filled with kids in a similar situation. She endured one flight delay after another until, finally, we received a call in the wee hours of the morning that she got the last seat on a flight heading to JFK Airport.

My husband suggested I fly to New York City the next morning to greet her at the airport. I was all in and felt an unusual calling to get on the flight in just hours. It was complicated; I would have to fly from Nashville to LaGuardia and then grab a taxi to JFK, as there were no direct flights.

When I landed, I felt the indescribable sense of not being alone. I will be bold and tell you that I was literally talking aloud to the Lord while walking the terminal, saying, "Father, I feel Your presence here. Lord, is Josiah here too? Because I just sensed a cloud of witnesses!" I was so excited not only to see Heather but also because something was up in the heavenlies. I assumed I was going to get to share the gospel or possibly lead someone to Christ. Thrilled at either idea, I continued out the terminal doors for the next leg of my journey.

As I waited in the cold for a taxi, I stood back by the sliding terminal doors, about thirty feet away from the curbside. I continued to visit with the Lord in my mind, praying for Heather and curious as to what He had planned, because I knew in my gut—there was something stirring.

It wasn't long before a black car pulled up to the curb and two beautiful women stepped out from the passenger side. In my mind, I told the Lord, *Oh, they know You! I can see it in their countenance.*

These women are my sisters! Then I saw a young man step out of the car from the other passenger side onto the street. As the car pulled away, I saw he was wearing fatigues. I prayed, *I have a son who serves in the military too, Father. Different, but he serves in Your military.*

The car had been directly in front of me, but the terminal door was to my right, so the women began to walk at an angle toward the door. However, the young man picked up his duffel bag and walked straight toward me. As he approached, we were both smiling from ear to ear. *He thinks I'm somebody else,* I thought. When he reached me, he set his bag down and hugged me!

That bear hug seemed to last an eternity, although I am certain it was closer to thirty seconds. I held him as tight as he held me. My eyes never closed, and as I glanced over his shoulder, I could see the women with him saying, "How sweet!" I was certain they thought I had approached him. *This feels holy, Lord,* I thought. *Am I right? This is about Siah, but I don't know what this is!*

Finally, I peeled away, and I said, "Thank you, buddy, and Merry Christmas." I remember he quietly said something, but I couldn't make it out. Possibly a simple "Merry Christmas" in return. He then picked up his bag and proceeded to walk into the terminal. The ladies lagged behind, staring and wondering. I asked them if he was one of their sons. One of the women said yes; the other was his aunt. I asked his name. "Clark," they replied. I explained that he had approached me, and I told them I'd be praying for Clark. I will never forget his kindness.

As a taxi pulled up and I jumped in, I continued to ask the Lord, *What was that?!* I knew He was shouting something to me, but it was too obvious to see just yet. Hours passed by as I waited for Heather at JFK. When at last she landed, my reunion with my daughter was filled with joy and nonstop chatter.

Finally, on the plane returning home to Nashville, when there was a moment to reflect, I shared the story with her. As I tried to solve the enigma, pondering, inquiring of the Lord, I heard, *You were asking for a hug, weren't you?* I couldn't believe it!

You see, during the hard days of this sad season we'd been in, I'd tearfully pray on my knees for a hug from Josiah. I've not met a mother of a child in Heaven who has not asked this very thing—but always and only hoping for a hug in a dream. I'd received a few hugs since Siah left, but I *never* imagined the glory of this one! The spontaneous, unexpected goodness of the Lord blew me away!

In the days that followed my holy encounter, I reasoned and reflected on the fullness of it all. First, God spoke to me about how Josiah was participating in some heavenly form of warfare and confirmed it via Philippians 1:6. Second, He led me to find the two pictures of Josiah wearing fatigues and told me to display them where I would see them. Third, He connected me to LaGuardia Airport for my providential encounter and gave me the sense that these strangers were followers of Christ (and truly, family!) even before my holy hug.

Guys, I received my hug from Josiah by proxy through Clark! We are one body, on both sides of the veil. We move and breathe together as one! I know Josiah and Jesus were there in the cloud, saying, "Here you go! Here is that hug you've been asking for!"

It is a beautiful mystery. Jesus, in His kindness, went so far out of His way to tend to this mother's heart in ways far beyond what

I could ask or imagine. Look at the passages below, one of which I quoted previously:

> For as we have many members in one body, but all the members do not have the same function, so we, being many, are one body in Christ, and individually members of one another. (Rom. 12:4–5)

> These things we also speak, not in words which man's wisdom teaches but which the Holy Spirit teaches, comparing spiritual things with spiritual. But the natural man does not receive the things of the Spirit of God, for they are foolishness to him; nor can he know them, because they are spiritually discerned. But he who is spiritual judges all things, yet he himself is rightly judged by no one. For "who has known the mind of the LORD that he may instruct Him?" But we have the mind of Christ. (1 Cor. 2:13–16)

This lesson on the body of Christ—the church, the Bride—has taught me that we are physically linked! We are His hands and feet! We have one purpose, and He has sent us out to be a part of answering prayer and ministry. We, according to His good pleasure, can be the answer to another person's prayer, participating in things far beyond this temporal world.

When I get to Heaven and see Clark one day, I can't wait to ask what compelled him to give me that hug. I'm convinced that at times we hear the Holy Spirit instructing and at other times we are simply compelled by God and find ourselves doing inspired things without a second thought. I think of John 10:27: "My sheep hear My voice, and I know them, and they follow Me."

If He who is greater is in me (see 1 John 4:4), then I am going to act according to His will more than to the flesh. We know we battle the enemy, but any good deed—a gesture of kindness, like a hug to a grieving mom—is on the Lord's radar. The joy of participating in these acts has put new wind in my sails. When prompted to encourage, compliment, hug, or share the gospel with a complete stranger, I seldom hesitate, because I know this could be exactly what the other person needs to survive today. In fact, this could be the answer to a saint's prayer in Heaven, praying for a lost child here on earth (see Rev. 8:3–4).

When I get to Heaven, I don't want to look back with regret over missed opportunities I had to engage with the body of Christ here on earth. Be courageous, fellow believer. You may be God's answer to a desperate prayer that will change the trajectory of a life!

Reflection

> And I am certain that God, who began the good
> work within you, will continue his work until it
> is finally finished on the day when Christ Jesus
> returns. (Phil. 1:6 NLT)

Remember, the good work Jesus began does not stop when life here on earth is done. It continues across the great divide. Make a list of the talents your loved one has—not *had*, but *has*. Ask the Lord to

help you recall conversations and details that highlight both person-
ality and gifting. Imagine the beauty of fulfilling that dear person's
destiny in an environment that is full of supernatural creativity and
excitement, with the Lord Himself cheering your loved one on.

If perhaps you've been struggling with worship and prayer,
I think this may be the right place to begin again. I very gently
encourage you to turn on some worship music or kneel in prayer.

chapter 7

the eagle

Does the hawk fly by your wisdom,
and spread its wings toward the south?
Does the eagle mount up at your command,
and make its nest on high?

Job 39:26–27

In October 2008, ten months before Josiah left for Heaven, I found myself preparing to teach at a women's retreat for the ladies at Grace Chapel, our church plant. Although my sidekick Donna and I had organized retreats for years, I never jumped at the opportunity to teach. However, there was something different about this year. After much prayer, I'd felt certain the Lord was directing me to share a story that might testify of His presence in our lives even before the day we say yes to Jesus as our Savior. I wanted to highlight His omniscience (infinite awareness) and His omnipresence (being everywhere at once)!

During this season, I had prayed for the Lord to remind me of things from my childhood—places and experiences I'd possibly forgotten. I found myself dreaming in delightful, intimate detail of things that had impacted my life. One night He gave me a vivid dream from when I was around four years old. I felt the morning fog at the beach where I'd spent my summers. I could smell the flowers on the way up the path to Pacific Coast Highway and feel the tiny fallen berries as they stuck to the bottoms of my little feet. I saw the stones on the path and heard the squeak when opening the wrought iron gate that led into the alley.

He showed me things about my life that only He would know, proving His ever-present all-knowingness! Apart from these reminders in the night, I would never have recalled the smells, the feelings, or the sounds in such fine detail. But you see, He was there walking along the path with me even as a small child. He knew the details because He is God of the details.

Those who know me would agree that I am quite the nature girl, as my dad raised my sisters and me to pay attention to the creation around us. Dad instilled a sort of awe in our hearts toward all things nature. Birds have always held a special fascination for me, so during this season, the Lord began speaking to me specifically about eagles. Truth is, I'd had several eagle sightings growing up, and they were unforgettable. Even at a young age, I was so very thankful to God for giving me these encounters. He reminded me that He was the One all along creating these moments. "Remember when you spotted the huge golden eagle while riding horses in the pasture? Remember the one standing beside the road? The dreams you've had about eagles? These were all designed by My hand."

A particularly vivid memory from my childhood was of lying on my back on my chartreuse shag carpet in 1971, at age ten, listening repeatedly to John Denver's song "The Eagle and the Hawk." Over and over, I'd pick up the needle on my hi-fi turntable and set it back down on the vinyl album. As I lay back, I'd envision an eagle soaring. My eyes would fill with tears, as even as a child, I was deeply touched by this song. It was as if God were speaking to me way back then, training me to pay attention. I know the lyrics by heart; here's how they begin:

> *I am the eagle, I live in high country*
> *In rocky cathedrals that reach to the sky.*[1]

John Denver did not claim to be a Christ follower; even so, the Holy Spirit used his lyrics to touch a ten-year-old girl long ago. *He* did because *He* can!

As I continued to prepare my testimony of God's faithfulness throughout our lives for the retreat, He made it clear that this teaching would be titled "A Sentimental Journey." The Lord would use my story to stir the other ladies' memories as well, to help them gain a fresh perspective and see His love and wooing even when they were still lost. Romans 5:8 says, "But God demonstrates His own love toward us, in that while we were still sinners, Christ died for us." God met me with Scripture to tie it all together with a bow, until one morning He went even further out of His way to prove this was certainly Him directing me in this teaching.

Gift from Above

As I sat at my computer, studying, I glanced out the window and spotted something curious in the yard. I'm that girl who notices when anything is askew in her surroundings. I can sense or see a shift to an unusual degree—a book out of place, a framed painting at just a slight tilt. I said aloud to the Lord, "Wait—is that what I think it is?"

I immediately got up and went outside to get a look. I'm sure the Lord took much delight in my expression, jaw dropped and eyes wide, as I picked up a huge feather that had been precisely placed within my view. Five acres of yard to choose from, and the Lord knew where I'd be and when. What a divine setup!

I picked up the feather, held it up, and said, "Okay, Lord. Even though I'm super excited about this, I am not going to assume this is an eagle feather. It could be a turkey feather as far as I know!" So I told Him the next time I saw my friend Brian, who is a nature expert from the area, working out on the land, I'd ask him.

A few days passed before I saw Brian. I quickly grabbed the feather and took it out for his inspection. "Bri, what kind of feather is this?"

His immediate response: "It's an eagle feather!"

"*What?* Brian, I've been studying eagles in the Word these past several weeks, and Jesus dropped an eagle feather for me! What type of eagle do you think it was?"

He replied, "A bald eagle!"

Our intimate Creator dropped a gift just for me, as if to say, "You're going the right direction with this, Sarah. Now just keep moving this way." I'd never have imagined that the sentimental journey the Lord would set me on would be a precursor to things He would show me when Josiah went to Heaven.

We all know Isaiah 40:31, which is an incredible promise, but verses 29–30 give us a much more intimate look at the recipients of Creator God's promise—to you and me, dear mom. To those who lie desperate, broken, and weak, this passage speaks to us:

> He gives power to the weak,
> And to those who have no might He increases
>   strength.
> Even the youths shall faint and be weary,
> And the young men shall utterly fall,
> *BUT* those who wait on the LORD
> Shall renew their strength;
> They shall mount up with wings like eagles,
> They shall run and not be weary,
> They shall walk and not faint. (vv. 29–31)

I set the eagle feather in an place where all could see, and I testified to my family. How amazing and good of our God. How kind of Him to give me an eagle feather!

I taught at that retreat in October 2008. Never would I have imagined that only ten months later, our son would be leaving for Heaven. I shared the feather with all who attended as physical evidence and a tangible witness of God's faithfulness. In obedience to something I felt the Lord telling me to do, I attempted to sing "The Eagle and the Hawk" at the close of my session—raw and a cappella. It was emotional and sad and hard for me, beyond what I'd have ever thought. I didn't really understand what was happening, but the

Holy Spirit was with me as I struggled to get even one word out of my mouth. I wept bitter tears through it all.

> He was already there in our future
> before our great sorrow struck.
> He is Immanuel, God with us—in
> our past, present, *and* future.

When reflecting back on this experience, I can see it was different from anything I'd experienced before—not your average tender moment. It was as if the Spirit in me was weeping toward my future. The deep grief unknown to me in the moment, He knew well was approaching. He was already there in our future before our great sorrow struck. He is Immanuel, God with us—in our past, present, *and* future (see Matt. 1:23).

It's evident today that God had been using eagles throughout my life to symbolize His presence. I'd never have imagined, however, that these experiences would heighten and continue with our Josiah leaving for Heaven. Only after Josiah flew did the reason become more fully known to me. In God's infinite wisdom, the Holy Spirit was drawing out my memories, and He would only continue to build on the "eagle" after our tragic day.

Ladies, the Father created you to soar! He knows every detail. He has been with you from the moment you were conceived. He is in the middle of your story. Wait on Him! He shall renew your strength!

Eagles' Wings

Months after Josiah went to Heaven, Josiah's friend Lucy called to share a dream that included all three of us. She unfolded the details like this:

"Sarah, you and I were standing at Five Points [a place in downtown Franklin], and there was a pretty good crowd. We looked across the street, and there was Josiah. He could see us, and we were the only ones who could see him. We then began walking toward each other. I said to you, 'Sarah, do you have the feather?' It was like I was asking, 'Do we have everything we need? Are we equipped and ready?' You said yes and pulled an eagle feather from your back pocket. Josiah didn't say a word, but he was smiling at us like he was happy that we were together. He then came and stood between the two of us, turned into a huge eagle, flapped his wings twice, and was gone. His wings were enormous. They were so powerful that they lifted him with just two swooshes."

I replied, "Oh my gosh, Lucy! First, earlier today I was totally meditating on a verse pertaining to eagles in the Word and was pondering the idea of Josiah flying in Heaven. Second, and what you'd never imagine, is that I *do* have an eagle feather! Like, who has an eagle feather?! Not very many, I think!" Wow, wow, wow. It was an amazing, synchronized manifestation of a powerful word! God sync!

In an act of obedience, I knew I was supposed to give the eagle feather to Lucy. It seemed evident that it was now hers because of its appearance in her dream. I reasoned in my heart that the next time she came over, I would pass it on. We were certain to talk about how the feather was a symbol for us—a part of our story. It was simple for me to release it to her because I'd not made it an idol. Rather, it would be a passing of a baton that symbolized a little piece of Siah and how he is living in the Kingdom. He is not an eagle—he is fully Josiah—but he *is* soaring.

This eagle theme continued to develop beyond finding the feather and Lucy's dream. The week after I gave the eagle feather to Lucy, I ran into our dear friends the Robinsons at Sunday service. Charles and Siouxanne are Native Americans who travel the States with their family, sharing Christ with Native peoples. Because of their heritage, they have a deep appreciation for how the Lord speaks through nature—and eagles in particular. Through the years, I'd shared with them about many dreams and sightings I'd experienced, and this day I told them about Lucy's dream. (I left out the part about the feather and passing it on to her.)

Without any prompting—save from the Holy Spirit—Charles welled up with tears. He said, "Sarah, I have had this in my Bible for seven years, waiting on the Lord for the right moment." He then slid out a large feather and said, "This is for you!" It was a golden eagle feather. According to Charles, eagle feathers are given to others in honor and are displayed with dignity and pride. They are handled with great regard.

We were both in tears as I received this sensational gift. Only in that moment did I tell Charles that I had in fact had a bald eagle feather that the Lord had given me, but days before I had given it to Lucy. "Charles, I just gave a feather away, and now the Lord is giving it back!" Neither of us could fully comprehend all He was saying in the moment, but it felt as if something huge was coming!

After the dream and the gift of the feather, I felt confident this was the Lord speaking, but I asked Him to please show my family it was *really* Him. At times they felt I was hyper-spiritualizing, so I wanted more confirmation for their sakes. I again prayed for a witness from Jesus.

One day, out of the blue—Thursday, June 23, 2011—my husband noticed the treads on my tires were worn. Who cares about tires when you're walking through grief? It seemed such a mundane thing when I was missing my son. Nonetheless, Steve took my car to be dropped off at a friend and fellow believer's tire shop. He left the keys and simply asked, "Could you just go ahead and get new tires on my wife's car? Her tires are bad, and we need new ones ASAP. I don't care which brand you choose."

The next morning, we went into the shop together to pick up the car. The store owner was behind the counter when we walked in, and without even a hello, he looked at me and said, "Well, you're with the eagles now!" I looked at Steve, thinking, *Have you been talking about my eagle experiences?* "What are you talking about?" I asked. His reply amazed me. He said, "You know? You'll mount up with wings as eagles. You're with the eagles now. I got you Goodyear Eagle tires. It was the craziest thing. They were the only tires I could find that would fit your car!"

Steve looked at me. In that moment I knew Jesus had made a way to answer my prayer for others to receive confirmation. To answer my seemingly trivial prayer, Jesus compassionately went out of His way to make sure Eagles were the only tires available!

A Special Visitor

The following day was a Saturday, and one of Josiah's friends was getting married at noon just two houses over from ours. I'd planned to wake early that morning and go to Target to pick up a wedding gift for the kids. I left the house filled with so much hope from my more thorough understanding of Heaven and the cloud of witnesses. How incredibly real it is and always has been—more and more so all the time.

At 10:30 a.m., I received a call from my daughter Heather. She was in tears, and of course this scared me. "Sis, what's the matter?"

"Mom, Aubrey kept barking, so I went outside to see what she was barking at. Mom, you won't believe what is on the roof of the house!"

"Sis, is there an eagle on the roof?"

"Yes, Mom, and it's enormous!"

"Oh my gosh, Sissy. I am heading home now."

Our home is approximately twelve minutes from where I was shopping. As I drove, I pondered: *Is it really an eagle? Is it possibly a buzzard? Will God, in His mercy, allow it to stay so I can see it too?* As I pulled up the driveway, my eyes became like saucers. The bird was enormous, and it was an *eagle*! A beautiful golden eagle! I'd never seen a golden eagle in Tennessee, so this was an added surprise. We all gathered outside to watch him. He remained on the roof for an hour and a half, finally flying away as the wedding began. We all saw him take off from two houses over. It was holy, majestic, and lavish of the Lord to send a sign so loud and clear.

As I asked the Lord throughout the day what He was saying, two things became evident. First, my husband said earlier that morning that he had asked the Lord for a God Nod that Josiah was somehow aware of his childhood friend getting married. Of course, our minds would go to a sunflower, rainbow, or something of this sort that held significance with our boy, but an eagle on our roof? This was next level. I told the Lord, "It seems as if You are shouting something from the rooftop! What is it, Father?"

Hours passed until out of the blue, I heard the Lord. He said, "On earth as it is in Heaven" (see Luke 11:2). Once again, at the speed of light, I knew exactly what He was shouting and that this was not just for our immediate family but for all to hear:

> I am giving you a physical example of how the saints live on Heaven's side of the veil. Did you see how the eagle never flinched? The buzzards were harassing him. The mockingbirds were dive-bombing him. The crows were scolding him the entire time he was up on the roof. The eagle merely looked to his right and to his left, but never once did he move even a foot. On this side of the veil, My followers will be harassed. You will be mocked. Death (symbolized by the buzzards) will circle you, but you need to hold your ground! Do not flinch. The war has been fought and victory already won. On earth, as it is in Heaven!

I was blown away! I'd never thought of that verse in the Lord's Prayer this way. How could I possibly imagine the beautiful symbolism God had set in motion to give us a physical display of what life looks like in the heavenly realm? Again, there are so many

layers to the living Word, and it continues to bring revelation far
beyond our expectations as we give ourselves more and more to
Him and His Word!

A few months into our Josiah leaving for Heaven, Jesus reminded me
of His own words: "Ye heard how I said to you, I go away, and I come
unto you. If ye loved me, ye would have rejoiced, because I go unto
the Father: for the Father is greater than I" (John 14:28 ASV). The
word *rejoice* here seems harsh. Really? Rejoice? The original Greek
for this word actually means to be of good cheer or to be happy.[2] I
can receive that much better than *rejoice*. The word for "love" here?
Agapaō, which means unconditional love.[3]

This is a hard one, friends and fellow moms, and I deliver these
words with the softest of tones. Consider this: since we love our
children unconditionally, coupled with a fuller understanding of
the grandeur and glory of Heaven, let's consider being joyful for
them. Am I right in assuming that every mother is happy when she
knows her child is happy? The more we can unconditionally love
our children and family of God in Heaven, the more we will see joy
restored to our own lives. Tears? Yes, of course. Joy doesn't vanquish
the emptiness and the sorrow. But agreeing to be joyful *for* them will
work toward patching the pain. Applying the pressure of this truth
will help stop the bleeding. The question is, Can you agree to be
joyful for them even in the midst of your deepest sorrow?

Friend, our sons and daughters are living their best lives in the
heavenlies. They are fighting for the Kingdom from a place of true

victory—not only knowing it by faith, but now living it by sight.
They know victory in its fullness, without the hindrance of fear,
anxiety, or the weight of this world. Why not live life on this side
just as your child is living on the other—in victory! Like the eagle,
do not flinch when you are mocked. Do not move when the Enemy
is harassing you. Stand your ground, as the cloud of witnesses looks,
hoping we will rise up in full faith. Never withdraw or give up spiritual territory!

> So do not throw away your confidence; it will be
> richly rewarded.
>   You need to persevere so that when you have
> done the will of God, you will receive what he has
> promised. For,
>
> > "In just a little while,
> > he who is coming will come
> > and will not delay."
>
> And,
>
> > "But my righteous one will live by faith.
> > And I take no pleasure
> > in the one who shrinks back."
>
> But we do not belong to those who shrink back
> and are destroyed, but to those who have faith and
> are saved. (Heb. 10:35–39 NIV)

Mothers, do not withdraw from the faith planted in you. Fight the good fight with a new, heavenly perspective. Fight like you're a mighty eagle on your rooftop. Hold your ground for the sake of your family, and don't give up! "Wait on the LORD; be of good courage, and He shall strengthen your heart; wait, I say, on the LORD!" (Ps. 27:14).

Ivan the Eagle

Some months passed, and Steve and I were invited to travel with some friends who had also suffered a family member leaving for Heaven. We were all walking in Nova Scotia one afternoon when Steve and I felt the sudden desire to split off from our group and take a different road. As we walked along the sidewalk, my eyes were drawn to some beautiful paintings on display in a window. I quickly said, "Honey, we need to go into this gallery."

As soon as we entered, my heart exploded with joy. We were surrounded by the most beautiful, colorful, whimsical display of paintings of various animals, most just of their faces. Then I turned to see the most magnificent painting of a bald eagle. As we talked with the women in the gallery, I briefly shared how the Lord spoke to me through eagles and how this painting felt significant. Melissa, the artist who was randomly in the gallery at that moment to finish her display, began the most precious conversation with me.

She was drawn to a pendant I wear daily and picked it up from around my neck for a closer look. She was suddenly inquisitive about our lives. "What is this?" she asked. "Is there a significance?"

"Yes," I replied, "The pendant is of our son Josiah. He went to Heaven in a single-car accident in 2009 at age nineteen."

Her eyes welled up with tears. She replied, "My brother Jared went to Heaven at that same age in a single-car accident too." Jesus was kindly knitting together the hearts of absolute strangers. As we shared our experiences, we learned more about Melissa, her love for Christ, and that her brother is also a believer. This entire conversation took place directly in front of the eagle painting and bore witness of how the Lord had spoken to Melissa concerning her brother through dreams and Scripture. It was beautiful!

As we stood there, my husband said something that I had honestly not even thought of—possibly it felt too extravagant. Steve said, "Don't you think this is our painting? It seems as if the Lord painted this through Melissa just for us."

"Wow! I think you're right!" I replied. As we inquired even more about the eagle, Melissa mentioned that she names all her animal paintings as the Lord inspires her. She said, "Your eagle is named Ivan, which means 'God is gracious.'"

This was such a gift. God is gracious indeed! In His providence, He sent us down a random road, sent the blessing of yet another eagle into our lives, and deemed his name "God Is Gracious"! Ivan is well-known within our family circle. He resides on a wall in our home where all can see. Melissa and I have stayed in touch all these years as we walk this road together, continually reminded that her brother Jared is wildly alive and soaring with our Josiah in the Kingdom that cannot be shaken!

P.S. The eagle sightings continue!

Reflection

Read Psalm 27.

Every mother is happy when she knows her child is happy. The more we unconditionally love our children in Heaven, the sooner our hearts will feel joy again.

Friend, in this moment, through both tears and joy, imagine your child, friend, or other loved one experiencing paradise. I realize the conflict, but I also know this truth brings freedom and restoration because when we know our children are happy, we are happy.

This is sacred and not to be approached as a school assignment, but if you feel God's strength, I propose that you consider writing a letter to your loved one—but with eternal eyes. Write as if he or she is on a mission trip abroad because—hear me now—it's the truth!

chapter 8

occupy

Whatever you do, work heartily, as for the
Lord and not for men, knowing that from the
Lord you will receive the inheritance as your
reward. You are serving the Lord Christ.

Colossians 3:23–24 ESV

Six years into this journey, the voice of the Lord whispered a word into my spirit that pierced my heart. This word was given gently, and the lesson it taught me eventually provided comfort, but my heart initially recoiled in disappointment. I didn't want to listen. I didn't want anything to do with it.

"*Occupy?* Did you say, 'Occupy'? Oh, Father, please don't say that!"

You see, and possibly you well know, the word *occupy* is a fearful thing to say to a mother walking through grief. When all you long for is the rapture and your heavenly reunion but then you hear the Lord say something that implies a longer wait … well, it brings a sting to the heart.

At the mere mention of the word *occupy*, you may also feel that sting. Stay with me! You too assume this word implies length of days, and to a grieving mom who longs to see her child's face, this seems agonizing. Why would God ask such a thing? Let's look at the definition of *occupy* to start unpacking what God was saying to me.

> *occupy* (verb)
>   1: to engage the attention or energies of
>   2: to take up (a place or extent in space)
>   3: to take or hold possession or control of
>   4: to reside in as an owner or tenant[1]

Taking up space and keeping oneself busy all allude to remaining longer. How in the world could this work for my good? Was it just me, or did this word and its concept affect others in the same way?

So I mentioned *occupy* to a few others who were walking in grief, including my daughters, Heather and Destiny. Without hesitation, when I mentioned that the Lord had spoken the word *occupy* to me, each responded with an expression of sadness, as if they had received disappointing news. One of them actually gasped! I had reacted the same way, but I resolved to inquire of the Lord a bit further. Surely, I wasn't understanding clearly.

I sat on this word and reasoned for a few days. In the meantime, I was reminded of the character and nature of Father God. He is kind. He is merciful. He corrects me with His gentle hand. He does not say anything that is not seasoned in love, and He has my best interest in mind. So what was He saying, and had I jumped to a negative conclusion because of my grief wound? Had I misinterpreted His intent?

I heard again, "Occupy until I come"—a phrase I knew well. It is pulled from the parable of the minas found in Luke's gospel (19:11–27 KJV). I began to search the Word. I love scouring through the Word. It's a joy to go further and deeper than just a casual read and, oh, the reward of finding hidden treasure! I began the search hoping the Lord had a surprise twist waiting for me—a special hook that He might be hanging on this verse. It felt as if I were peeking around the corner to see a hint of what I'd find. I was a bit fearful at the start, but I'd reasoned enough through the process to ultimately realize He meant this word to spur me on, as I'd felt stalled in my vision and passion for quite a while.

At this time, I had been mostly reading from the King James Version. It seemed fitting that in my search for the word *occupy* within this translation, it only appeared twice in the entire Bible. And more specifically, it appeared just once in the New Testament, in this exact passage.

It meant that much more to me that the Lord had spoken a very specific word that isn't frequently used in the King James Version. It's as if He were saying, "Look at this! Look right here and don't be distracted." He eliminated the potential of going any other direction in His Word. I told the Lord, "I know You wouldn't speak this to me with any intent of bringing further despair. So why, Lord?" In studying the parable, it became evident His heart was to bring encouragement, *not* discouragement!

Before I unpack the parable of the minas, let's look at the passage itself:

And as they heard these things, he added and spake a parable, because he was nigh to Jerusalem, and because they thought that the kingdom of God should immediately appear.

He said therefore, A certain nobleman went into a far country to receive for himself a kingdom, and to return.

And he called his ten servants, and delivered them ten pounds, and said unto them, Occupy till I come.

But his citizens hated him, and sent a message after him, saying, We will not have this man to reign over us.

And it came to pass, that when he was returned, having received the kingdom, then he commanded these servants to be called unto him, to whom he had given the money, that he might know how much every man had gained by trading.

Then came the first, saying, Lord, thy pound hath gained ten pounds.

And he said unto him, Well, thou good servant: because thou hast been faithful in a very little, have thou authority over ten cities.

And the second came, saying, Lord, thy pound hath gained five pounds.

And he said likewise to him, Be thou also over five cities.

And another came, saying, Lord, behold, here is thy pound, which I have kept laid up in a napkin:

For I feared thee, because thou art an austere man: thou takest up that thou layedst not down, and reapest that thou didst not sow.

And he saith unto him, Out of thine own mouth will I judge thee, thou wicked servant. Thou knewest that I was an austere man, taking up that I laid not down, and reaping that I did not sow:

Wherefore then gavest not thou my money into the bank, that at my coming I might have required mine own with usury?

And he said unto them that stood by, Take from him the pound, and give it to him that hath ten pounds.

(And they said unto him, Lord, he hath ten pounds.)

For I say unto you, That unto everyone which hath shall be given; and from him that hath not, even that he hath shall be taken away from him.

But those mine enemies, which would not that I should reign over them, bring hither, and slay them before me. (Luke 19:11–27 KJV)

As we break down this parable to see what we can glean from it, it is vital that we remember the why. Verse 11 makes it absolutely clear: Jesus needed to address the issue at hand. Those around Him assumed the Kingdom of God would immediately appear. He needed to communicate the truth to them in His divine way and in the common people's language and culture.

I can personally relate to this mindset. Two thousand years after Christ's resurrection, I too expect His imminent return to establish His Kingdom. Jesus gives this hope in the lives of the grieving, and it is His will that we all live in the knowledge that He could return at any moment. But it's equally important that we live with intention the days He has given us here on earth. We don't want to be like those who said, "Where is the promise of his coming? for since the fathers fell asleep, all things continue as they were from the beginning of creation" (2 Pet. 3:4 KJV).

The nobleman in this parable is Christ, who is leaving to acquire a kingdom and then will return, just as Jesus has acquired His Kingdom and will soon return. The nobleman called ten servants and gave each one a mina (or one pound) to invest while he was gone. He showed no partiality, and each was given the potential to make eternal investments that would bring reward upon the nobleman's return.

But the citizens hated the nobleman and said he would not reign over them. This is the spirit of those in the world even now. They are not at all concerned with eternity, and they hate God. They resent the idea of anyone having any authority over them. Take note, there is a difference between being a citizen, a part of the general population, and a servant in the house of the Lord.

The nobleman then returned and inquired about his servants (followers). He wanted to see how they had invested the minas.

There will be an account required upon Jesus' return. It is His hope that we, the servants, will make much of our time because He is in fact returning and will reward those who steward their gifts well.

For the one servant who didn't invest his gift, it was taken away and given to the servant whose mina had multiplied ten times. It is of utmost importance that we understand the heart of the nobleman (Jesus). I believe the servant, in saying, "because thou art an austere man," was just making up an excuse for having been lazy or perhaps apathetic. That behavior does not please God, as He is looking for those who will trust Him and join in on Kingdom activity and adventure. Galatians 6:9 says, "Let us not grow weary while doing good, for in due season we shall reap if we do not lose heart."

Jesus told this parable to the people specifically because He knew they were assuming that His Kingdom was going to be set up immediately. He needed them to not lose heart and so communicated to them that He'd be leaving but would return at a later time to establish His Kingdom here on earth. And ladies, let's not forget there is a reason for His delay. Second Peter 3:9 says, "The Lord is not slack concerning His promise, as some count slackness, but is longsuffering toward us, not willing that any should perish but that all should come to repentance."

In the leaving, however, He gave us minas to invest, a purpose to occupy our days. Proverbs 29:18 says, "Where there is no vision, the people perish" (KJV). This investment enlarges the Kingdom, yes! But Jesus knew His followers would need vision or we would perish! He knew that *I* needed assignments to keep me from becoming dormant and dull while waiting for His return.

> Grieving mom, grieving friend:
> Occupy until He comes!
> Press on toward the goal!

The Lord then told me, "Sarah, it is about the one thing! That one mina! What is your one thing, Sarah? That thing you know well that I have been pointing you to? That thing that at the hearing of this word, you know I have assigned you to do?"

What was mine? Apart from the obvious and absolute call to my family and church ministry, I knew that one thing pressing on me was to write. To write these very pages.

I'd been lazy and full of excuses and a bit of fear, to be honest. I was procrastinating with the one mina He had very personally given me. I'd sat without moving to follow His lead for close to two years even after I had received crystal-clear confirmation. "Where from here, Lord?" I asked. I repented of being lazy. The idea was striking to me, as I am always up on my feet, doing something (I would never be accused of being lazy!), yet I had neglected to do the "one thing" He had assigned to me.

Paul wrote about the one thing in Philippians 3:12–15:

> Not that I have already attained, or am already perfected; but I press on, that I may lay hold of that for which Christ Jesus has also laid hold of me. Brethren, I do not count myself to have apprehended; but *one thing* I do, forgetting those things

which are behind and reaching forward to those
things which are ahead, I press toward the goal for
the prize of the upward call of God in Christ Jesus.

Therefore let us, as many as are mature, have
this mind; and if in anything you think otherwise,
God will reveal even this to you.

I've learned throughout my life the blessedness of living intentionally and the true gift of living with few regrets. The Lord in His
gentle guiding reminds me of this daily as I sit and type out these
stories. I do not want to be the wicked, lazy servant who didn't invest
in the Kingdom in whatever way possible. We should all live with
the ever-present desire to never miss a thing!

Grieving mom, grieving friend: Occupy until He comes! Press
on toward the goal!

*Please, Father, make Your plans and purposes for us so obvious that
we will never miss an opportunity! May we never live with that regret.
Thank You, God, for being so patient with my procrastination!*

As the Lord continued to minister to me and show me the error
of my original thinking around this word *occupy*, He reminded me
that by occupying, we actually hasten the day of His coming! Do
you hear that? We participate in speeding up the times. Second Peter
3:11–13 says:

What manner of persons ought you to be in holy
conduct and godliness, looking for and hastening
the coming of the day of God, because of which
the heavens will be dissolved, being on fire, and the

elements will melt with fervent heat? Nevertheless
we, according to His promise, look for new heavens
and a new earth in which righteousness dwells.

In verse 12, "looking for and hastening the coming of the day
of God" means anticipating the day and speeding it up! So, you see,
it is right to be watching and anticipating that grand reunion. Many
verses remind us to stay focused on that very thing, but coupled with
this is the hastening, the working, the *occupying* that we are called
to, to speed up the process.

"Occupy, Sarah!" My Father God, with that once-frightening
phrase, put wind in my sails again and brought movement and mission back to this vessel. These pages are the one thing in this season
that He wanted me to steward. This is my one mina, my occupation
and opportunity until that day. May I ask, what is your one mina,
your one thing? Pray, identify, and invest! You'll reap the most beautiful reward.

As I wait for my King's return, occupying until He comes,
I pray that my children, grandchildren, and possibly even future
great-grandchildren will find that one thing in each season to invest
into the Kingdom! Even so, come quickly, Lord Jesus!

Reflection

We need vision or we will perish. Without a vision, you will become
stagnant as you await Christ's return. Is there one thing that has
crossed your mind time and time again? A potential divine assignment that could help awaken your soul? Reading a particular book?
Volunteering at a local ministry? Planting a garden? Painting a wall?

Inquire of the Lord, and then, sister, I encourage you to step out in obedience. Remember, just "one" thing. I am betting you'll be delighted in what you find.

Jot down some ideas that have stirred in your heart. Go back to this list on occasion and ask, "What next, Lord?"

chapter 9

the wren

The LORD is close to the brokenhearted;
he rescues those whose spirits are crushed.

Psalm 34:18 NLT

Early one morning in the fall of 2016, as I sat on my front porch spending time with the Lord, I inquired of Him concerning an upcoming women's event at church. We had assigned different ladies from the congregation to speak, and I asked Him if He had something for me to share. Honestly, I usually look for a way out of speaking, but I always want to be obedient. If He speaks a word to share, then I am all in!

As I was processing the question, I heard an all-too-familiar thump on the window just feet away. I quickly glanced to my left, and there on the porch lay a stunned Carolina wren. Without a thought, I went out and scooped the wren into my hands. As I knelt on the porch, I prayed for the poor bird. Almost immediately, I heard the Lord say, "I am near the brokenhearted."

I continued to pray in the Spirit over the sweet bird and to breathe warm air onto his body as he lay in my cupped hands. In my experience (this has happened before!), within a minute or two, most birds will fly away, but not this guy. He was in pretty bad shape. His eyes were mostly closed, and when they finally opened, he appeared dazed and confused. There were moments when I thought he'd taken his last breath. Finally, he began to straighten his legs and get some balance. I opened my hands and off he flew.

He landed not far from my sight, and my instinct was to run and find him safety. As I looked around the corner, my cat had already (in a matter of a few seconds) taken him in his mouth. I commanded him to release the bird, and he quickly dropped him. Thankfully, the wren was still breathing, and there wasn't a spot of blood.

I swooped him up a second time, praying over him again, and he finally flew and took refuge under a bush. This time, I put my cat as far away as possible—anything I could do to give the poor bird a chance of survival.

As I reflected on what had just transpired, I immediately sensed this was no coincidence—in the same moment I was asking the Lord if He had something for me to say, these events unfolded in God's synchronicity. When something happens like this, I call it "God sync." Indeed, He spoke again: "I am near the brokenhearted." I knew the phrase God was referencing, so I grabbed my Bible and flipped to Psalm 34:18, which says, "The Lord is close to the broken-hearted; he rescues those whose spirits are crushed" (NLT).

Just as I immediately swept the bird into my hands, so does He scoop us up! When we are met with tragic circumstances, the Lord is there, ready to pick us up and comfort us. He gives us the unexplainable ability to live and press through sorrow by supernaturally blanketing us with a holy calm and a peaceful quiet. In the aftermath of trauma, it is best we lie limp in His everlasting arms and just breathe, just remain, just weep. I have literally felt His presence like a breath on my cheek—His Spirit can be that near and that rich in the midst of suffering. God breathes warmth and peace into our very souls. He is willing for us to stay there as long as we need—to rest, recover, and regain our strength while huddled in His safe place—until we are strong enough to stand again.

I'm reminded of John 14:26–27, in which Jesus foretold the comfort and peace the Holy Spirit would provide for Christ's followers: "But the Comforter, even the Holy Spirit, whom the Father will send in my name, he shall teach you all things, and bring to your remembrance all that I said unto you. Peace I leave with you; my peace I give unto you: not as the world giveth, give I unto you. Let not your heart be troubled, neither let it be fearful" (ASV).

From my experience, there is a period of time after trauma when we feel as if we're almost walking in a fog—at times hazy on details and yet given a grace that is hard to put into words. It is God with us. With this grace comes the ability to survive what would otherwise crush one's soul. The medical field may deem this condition "shock," but I refuse to give the world any credit for something that can supernaturally reach beyond what man can touch—God's comfort! It's His kindness that shields us from the full sorrow until we are able to fully process and grieve.

Know this, beloved: the Enemy of your soul is like my cat, crouching at the door and ready to kill, steal from, and destroy you (see John 10:10). He is relentless, and in our most vulnerable moments, he will try to pick us off … *but* God! Our Abba Father is there to deliver us, pull us out of the snare, bind up our wounds, and set us free. The Enemy may crouch at the door in an attempt to stop us, but he doesn't know who he is dealing with! We are God's kids, people who know their heavenly Father, and we will not retreat from the call of Christ.

> Our Abba Father is there to deliver us, pull us out of the snare, bind up our wounds, and set us free.

Later that day, I asked the Lord if this was a word He wanted me to share. As I've explained, this is my habit, since the Lord instructs us in the Word to check all things to make sure they are of a right spirit. As fruitful as it seemed to me personally, I needed confirmation from Him that this was for the ladies at the conference too.

Two days passed, and I came across the most amazing witness while thumbing through Instagram. My sister Liza, whom I'd not spoken to for a few weeks, had posted some of her beautiful art on her account. There in front of me was a watercolor painting of a Carolina wren with the same verse painted underneath: "The Lord is close to the brokenhearted"! There was the witness I needed—my confirmation that it was indeed His will for me to share the story. God impressed upon me to share that I was broken like that wren after Josiah went to Heaven. He whispered to me, "Look at you now! I was with you then, I'm with you now, and I'll be with these women too."

Two months later, I told the story to the ladies at the conference. Because I'd had my phone handy and filmed most of the bird's recovery that day, we projected the video of the wren in my hands on the screen behind me. Then I finished my talk by putting Liza's art on the screen. It all came together to bear witness to the women gathered that God speaks through whatever means He deems profitable—an injured bird, a piece of art, a hug from a random stranger, a dream, a vision, or the time of day—and He confirms it through His Word. He is always speaking, and we need to pay attention.

I could hear women weeping in the congregation. At His lead, I asked anyone to stand who could identify with being brokenhearted so we could circle around them to pray. They stood, we swooped them up, and we saw His comfort come.

Remember, God is both omniscient and omnipresent—He knows we need reassurance that He's near when we're brokenhearted. So let me assure you: He is near! Just lean into Him, trust, and watch Him show up (maybe in an unexpected way!).

I do want to caution you to stay far, far away from manipulating or overreaching to create confirmation in your flesh. Wait on the Lord, and don't unintentionally force circumstances that you want to see. Proverbs 3:5 says, "Trust in the LORD with all your heart, and lean not on your own understanding." Ask Him to confirm what He's telling you in a way that lets you know you've not manufactured a sign based on your own motivation.

There was a final chapter to the story that I didn't feel compelled to share at the conference. It was a sugar-on-top moment that occurred a few weeks after I'd held the sweet bird in my hands. One morning, as I sat reading, I heard a little pitter-patter

on the entry floor of our home. As I stood to investigate, I was
tickled to find that a Carolina wren had come inside our open
door and was dancing around on the floor. Was it the same one I
had rescued?! I can't say for certain, but when I approached him,
he flew up onto our foyer chandelier. *Oh no!* I thought. *How am I
going to get him out?*

Then a still, small voice reminded me that Carolinas are pretty
smart birds. *Just open the door, and he will find the way.* So I propped
the front door wide open, and a moment later, he flew to freedom.

I felt I could learn so much from my moment with that little
guy. The Lord reminded me, "He was a smart bird. He saw the door
and he took it. He knew the way out and didn't hesitate." We should
do the same and not play games or delay what we know will make
for peace! Go to the door. Go to Jesus! He is the door!

God gently used these two experiences with the wren to speak
to my heart. If He cares this much for a wren, how much more does
He care for us? (See Matt. 6:26; 10:29.) When we are brokenhearted,
God is near. His everlasting arms are ready to bind up our wounds
and nurture us back to health (see Deut. 33:27). And when we feel
stuck and need a way of escape, Jesus is the door through which we
run (see John 10:7–9). He's our ticket to freedom, our source of hope
and strength! He's our healer *and* our deliverer!

Do you need reassurance that He is here? I hope my intimate
journey is helping to prove His presence in your own personal story.
I pray you are grasping along with me how very intentional, personal,
real, and near He is in our deepest pain. May this book be a witness
to the fact that the Creator of all things has not left us alone. And one

day when our eyes are seeing clearly and we are once again steady on our feet, we will say, "God was indeed near!"

> For this reason I bow my knees to the Father of our Lord Jesus Christ, from whom the whole family in heaven and earth is named, that He would grant you, according to the riches of His glory, to be strengthened with might through His Spirit in the inner man, that Christ may dwell in your hearts through faith; that you, being rooted and grounded in love, may be able to comprehend with all the saints what is the width and length and depth and height—to know the love of Christ which passes knowledge; that you may be filled with all the fullness of God. (Eph. 3:14–19)

Reflection

> Peace I leave with you, My peace I give to you; not as the world gives do I give to you. Let not your heart be troubled, neither let it be afraid. (John 14:27)

Has the Enemy tried to guilt you out of peace? Has he whispered, "If you really loved the person you lost, you wouldn't sleep at night. You wouldn't have any joy"? The Enemy will try to rob us of all the good Jesus offers—and through the wiliest of ways. Receive Christ's peace. His peace makes no sense to the world, but it fits perfectly in His Kingdom.

Take a moment to sit with the Father. Ask Him to reveal thoughts or patterns that have prevented His peace. Identify them and write them down. Now, memorize the passage below, and apply it to those thoughts when they rise up.

> For the weapons of our warfare are not carnal but mighty in God for pulling down strongholds, casting down arguments and every high thing that exalts itself against the knowledge of God, bringing every thought into captivity to the obedience of Christ, and being ready to punish all disobedience when your obedience is fulfilled. (2 Cor. 10:4–6)

chapter 10

the divine script

And He began to say to them, "Today this
Scripture is fulfilled in your hearing."
Luke 4:21

In the Word we see the prophets of old declaring great acts of God, and then in His providential and most effective time, it all comes together and Jesus fulfills His divine script. The Spirit gave Jesus the anointing, or the supernatural, unique ability, to do the work He had been called to do. For example, Isaiah spoke prophetically about Jesus some seven hundred years before His birth. The second act was played out in these verses in a synagogue in Nazareth, His hometown, when Christ opened the scroll, read the verses, and proclaimed their fulfillment.

"The Spirit of the Lord is upon Me,
Because He has anointed Me
To preach the gospel to the poor;
He has sent Me to heal the brokenhearted,
To proclaim liberty to the captives

And recovery of sight to the blind,

To set at liberty those who are oppressed;

To proclaim the acceptable year of the LORD."

Then He closed the book, and gave it back to the attendant and sat down. And the eyes of all who were in the synagogue were fixed on Him. And He began to say to them, "Today this Scripture is fulfilled in your hearing." So, all bore witness to Him, and marveled at the gracious words which proceeded out of His mouth. And they said, "Is this not Joseph's son?" (Luke 4:18–22)

Even in our own lives, God is writing the next page. Our stories may be filled with twists and turns, but in the end His goal is healing, deliverance, sight, and liberty!

Let's stop and think about this for a moment and apply it to our own very specific wounds, whether grief, disappointment, or extreme loss. That Jesus was "anointed," in today's language, might sound like this: "Jesus has the chops" or "He's an expert." Jesus has the complete and perfect ability and authority to do whatever He wants by whatever means to fulfill all He declares in the above passage. Everything is at His disposal to fulfill His call, whether that be inside or outside the box some have put around His power. He has what it takes, period.

What is your need? If you're not quite certain, He is! He can pinpoint which issue needs attention and what it will take to bring you healing and encouragement. Then He will set out to create a divine script, or, because He is all-knowing, He has probably already created the script. And then, in a most unexpected, holy moment, the script is played out and—*bam*—you're face to face with encouragement so divine, it's beyond your imagination.

He'll bring good news to heal our broken hearts. He will free those who may be living as captives to regret or guilt. He will teach us how to see or regain eternal perspective. He will restore and bring hope. Jesus can do it. We serve a God who is all about second acts and next chapters. He's got the chops. *Oh yes, He does.*

Allow me to share some divine scripts from my own story. You'll come to see how God is about second acts—and then some. There seems to be no end to the beautiful things He does. This first story began just a few weeks after Josiah left for Heaven, when the Lord chose to answer a grieving mother's daring request.

> He'll bring good news to heal our broken hearts. He will free those who may be living as captives to regret or guilt. He will teach us how to see or regain eternal perspective. He will restore and bring hope. Jesus can do it.

Gone Fishing

After dropping Destiny, our youngest, off at school, I would often speak aloud to the Heavens. Because Hebrews 12:1 speaks of our being surrounded by a great cloud of witnesses, I felt the freedom to speak aloud to Siah and Jesus. It was healing to me to think that Josiah *might* hear—and to solidly know that Jesus absolutely *did* hear. I would hold back my tears all the way to Destiny's school and let them go the moment she and I had said our goodbyes. I would then desperately spill my thoughts and questions out to Jesus, stretching my arm across the passenger seat, saying, "I am holding your hand in the Spirit, Siah, and I have questions. Jesus, I have big questions.

"I want to know what you are doing, Josiah. I need to be somehow involved in your life even now, even in Heaven. I know you are doing Kingdom work, and I want to somehow be involved and finish what you started here.

"Father, You know what is best for me to know, and so because of Your great mercy, I am asking You this question: What is Josiah doing now? I believe that after nineteen years with my child, You wouldn't say, 'No, Sarah, you may not know.' That is not who I have known You to be, Father. So here I am, asking."

I received no immediate answer to my bold question, but I learned to wait on the Lord, to trust Him in every quiet place, to pour out my grief to Him, and to allow Him to be near to the brokenhearted. Remember, He came to heal the brokenhearted. I learned to excavate His Word in ways like never before. His Word became literal life to my bones. I ached to be close to Jesus, knowing He was "a Man of sorrows and acquainted with grief" (Isa. 53:3).

During this time, I settled in my heart that if for some reason it was not beneficial for me to know about Josiah's activities in Heaven, I would surrender to that. However, the ask still burned within me, and I truly believed God would somehow answer the cry of my heart as a mother in His way and in His time. But never would I have imagined how.

What follows is an entry from my journal.

On a Sunday I will never forget—October 25, 2009—a friend named Sammi approached Steve and me after our eleven o'clock service and said he needed to speak with us urgently. We met Sammi about a year and a half ago, when an Iraqi girl and her mother stayed with us while the little girl received medical care in Nashville. Sammi and his wife, Zainab, had served as live-in interpreters for them. During this time, Sammi became a close family friend, with he and Josiah developing a special bond.

As Steve and I sat down across from an obviously nervous Sammi, we could see from his face that he had something major to share. He explained this experience in the best language he could. He told us he'd had a dream about Josiah. Yet it was more than a dream and very real. So with tears in his eyes and trembling hands, Sammi began to unfold the dream:

> Steve and Sarah, I was riding in a car with you and Destiny, and we were heading for the lake. It was close, but it took a long time to get there. When we arrived, we began walking on the beach. I asked Steve, "Is this the sea or a lake? I cannot see to the other side. Why are we here?"

Steve answered, smiling, "Well, someone said it's a good place to be."

Then Sarah said, "Des and I are going to explore the other side of the beach." With this, Sarah and Destiny left the dream.

Steve was facing the sea, and I was behind him, observing. Steve said to me, "Sammi, we need to be leaving soon." I realized that the sun was going to set soon, and we needed to climb a hill to get back to the car so we could leave before dark. At this point, Josiah came walking up from Steve's right, and he was facing the sea. He was carrying a fishing pole. Josiah and Steve said a casual hello, as if they had not been apart.

Then Josiah said, "Dad, I don't want to leave. I want to stay and fish."

Steve answered, "Josiah, you don't know how to fish."

Josiah replied, "Yeah, I know. But I met this Guy, and He is teaching me how." Josiah then pointed the opposite way, and we turned to look. There was a Man in a robe who lifted a staff and nodded to confirm that He was the Man they were speaking about.

"Okay, Josiah, you can stay," answered Steve.

Josiah replied, "Yeah, Dad, there are a lot of hungry people and a lot of fishing that needs to be done."

Steve asked, "Where are all the people?"

Josiah answered, "Dad, you know what I mean."

Then Steve and Josiah said their goodbyes, and Josiah happily picked up his pole and bounded back down to the beach. He was visibly happy.

The dream continued. I became upset with Steve because I believed this was his opportunity to bring Josiah home. Then we started walking uphill to the car. I began to pull on Steve's shirt and asked him, "Where are we anyhow? And what is going on?"

I turned for one last look at the lake and saw several people fishing. They were visiting and laughing as they cast their lines. The sun was touching the water, and I could see that it was brilliant and bright where Josiah fished.

Steve never answered my question. He didn't even take a second look at the lake, but he did turn and give me a knowing smile.

We were absolutely blown away with what Sammi was sharing with us. Our eyes were filled with tears and wonderment. He wasn't quite finished. He then told us that the minute he awoke from the dream, he woke up Zainab and asked her to run and get him a glass of water, because he felt he had just been climbing and was extremely thirsty. He felt physically exhausted.

I asked, "Sammi, do you know what Jesus says about making us fishers of men?"

He replied, "I don't know anything the Bible says about fishing. All I know is that the boy [in another dream] had the dream about Josiah leaving the hospital room with God, and I remember thinking, 'What happens now in Josiah's life?' I am a Muslim, but I believe God gave me this dream because you are my family. I wondered where Josiah is and what he is doing now, and I thought you both must wonder too."

At this point Sammi looked directly into my eyes and said, "I want you to know, Sarah: Josiah has a job, and Josiah fishes."

Imagine my wide-eyed wonder when Sammi delivered the very direct answer to my very bold ask! I knew earlier as he was sharing the dream that it was certainly the answer, but specifically telling me Josiah has a job blew me away! *Are you kidding?*

Later, we continued to unfold the Scriptures to Sammi to help him understand what the dream meant: humanity is the sea, God Himself is the light, and Christians who live in Heaven are still active in Kingdom work, as God wills it, as evidenced by the fishing. We also shared that the Kingdom of Heaven is like his description of traveling to the lake: it is nearby—just on the other side of a very thin veil—but far away in the sense that we remain on this side until the day we cross over into eternity. Also, the Word speaks about Heaven being in the hearts of believers (see Luke 17:21) but also far away. (It won't be fully realized until Jesus sets up His Kingdom on the new earth in Revelation 21.)

The image of Jesus teaching Josiah how to fish and how to feed hungry people aligns perfectly with something Jesus told His disciples He came to do: make them fishers of men (Matt. 4:19). Although we don't fully understand the details of how or in what

way, we believe Josiah is participating in the catching of unbelievers
for Jesus Christ. (In an altar call after Josiah left for Heaven and
prior to sharing Sammi's story publicly, one young man told us,
"Your son has caught me.")

After two weeks of waiting for an answer, Creator God answered
my ask. Isn't that incredible? The Lord answered my outlandish, bold
question and subsequently was wooing a nonbeliever to Himself. My
friend Sammi was carrying the same question in his own heart that
I carried: *What is Josiah doing in Heaven?* He didn't physically ask
the Lord his question, but the Lord knows the hearts of men, and
He chose in His wisdom to answer us both through Sammi's dream.

And if that weren't enough, the Lord had more in store.… Eight
years later, my husband and I would have the opportunity to finish
the work that our son began with this friendship.

Now, you may be wondering while reading this account
of Sammi's dream why in the world God would choose to use a
Muslim man who has zero biblical knowledge to deliver a message
about Heaven and Josiah. This is not the first time God has used
unbelievers to deliver important messages. And more importantly,
this is not the first time He has used dreams to draw unbelievers to
Himself. When God wanted to announce the birth of his Son, He
did not just appear to the local shepherds outside Bethlehem. No,
He hung a bright star in the vast sky and planted the idea in the
hearts of three pagan wise men to make a life-changing journey.
They followed this star because they believed it would lead them to
the King of the Jews. And later, God again used these men, warning
them in a dream not to return to Herod and disclose Jesus' location
(see Matt. 2:1–12). And Pilate's wife received a message from God in

a dream that her husband should not participate in Jesus' trial and crucifixion (see Matt. 27:17–20).[1]

Gone Fishing: Part 2

> The Lord isn't really being slow about his promise, as some people think. No, he is being patient for your sake. He does not want anyone to be destroyed, but wants everyone to repent. (2 Pet. 3:9 NLT)

Hold on! The story continues. In the past decade Zainab received Christ, and yet our dear Sammi put off making a decision. I can't recall how many times I asked him why he was delaying, because he was obviously so happy at the mention of Jesus. Literally, Sammi would try not to smile at the mention of His name. It was as if he knew this Jesus already but just wasn't allowing himself to surrender. I recall in our kitchen about four years ago almost joking and with a smile saying, "Sammi, it is so obvious that you know the truth. When, buddy, are you going to just say yes?"

Then, eight years after his first dream, Sammi approached me at one of our church's Christmas services. I could tell by his body language that there was something pressing on him. "What is it, Sammi?" I inquired. He told me that he had had another dream with Josiah and that he needed to talk to us as soon as possible. He knew there was a risk involved because sharing would mean he was accountable to us to finally make a decision. Here is that encounter in Sammi's own words:

> I had another dream with Josiah, and I knew
> this time I had to make a choice. You're my close
> friends, and I knew you'd want to hear about my
> dream because of seeing and talking to Josiah.
>
> In the dream I was sitting in your bonus room
> when Josiah walked through the door. I didn't say
> a word, but Josiah walked right up to me and said,
> "Sammi, when are you going fishing with me?"
> Instead of answering, I stood up and walked out
> of the room.

I responded, "Sammi, you know what he means, right? You know Siah is asking, 'When are you going to say yes to Jesus?'" Sammi answered, "I know this is what he is asking. I don't know why I keep walking away." After church, Steve and I set up a time for the following night for Zainab and Sammi to come over for dinner and conversation. I remember the next day feeling an absolute confidence that *this* was the day Sammi would say yes to Jesus. My heart was bursting with hope at the idea that the Lord would use our son Josiah, who now lives in Heaven, in a dream to "fish" for Sammi. It was fascinating to me.

On December 18, 2017, Sammi and Zainab came over for dinner. There, at our dining room table, Sammi opened up more than ever before about his life experiences. He told us that because of trauma in Baghdad and things he had been exposed to as a child, he wanted nothing to do with any god—Muslim or Christian. But that night, through tears, Sammi made the decision to stop running and instead trust Jesus for his eternal salvation. Never had I heard such a real prayer and, oh, the tears. We were all a glorious mess.

When we reached out to Sammi the following morning, he testified that he was changed! We could hear the joy and hope in his voice. Still our friends to this day, Sammi and Zainab are forever family, and we will one day live forever together in Heaven. Now Sammi in turn is a fisher of men.

Can you see? Jesus is anointed! He is able to preach the gospel, heal the brokenhearted, deliver captives, open eyes to see, and bring hope in ways that are beyond our thinking to those who are bruised. Even through dreams.

Saints Are Aware

Before unpacking the next divine script, I want to share some biblical foundation. The question is frequently asked by those of us who have loved ones in Heaven, "Are they aware of what is going on down here on earth? Are they concerned with the state of people in general and especially family members living on the earth?" The answer is a balanced yes.

In a sermon some years ago, Greg Laurie said, "People in eternity are aware of the fact that loved ones are not saved. This is based on Luke 16.... In the afterlife we are the same person with real memories of earth. You will know more in heaven than you will on earth, not less. We don't ... [forget everything] when we go to glory." He also reminds us that "when people come to believe in Jesus it's 'public knowledge in heaven.'"[2]

In Luke 16:19–31, Jesus tells of the rich man and Lazarus, which addresses to a degree what those in eternity may know about family and friends on earth. The story tells how both the rich man and Lazarus left for eternity on the same day. Lazarus went to Heaven and the rich man to hell. The rich man wanted the Lord to send word to his brothers of the truth so they wouldn't go to hell also. God responded that if they didn't believe the prophets of old, then they wouldn't believe Him either; the point being, there is a knowing. The rich man in hell could recall his family as they were when he was alive, and he knew they didn't believe. He had only memory, not an awareness of the current affairs on earth.

Lazarus, on the other hand, although not speaking in this particular story, would have had a degree of knowing and an awareness of happenings with humanity in real time. We know from Scripture that all of Heaven rejoices when one sinner repents (see Luke 15:10). Jesus said in John 8:56 that Abraham rejoiced to see His day, meaning Abraham from Heaven rejoiced to see the day of Jesus' birth on earth.

In Luke 9:30–31 Moses and Elijah, who had passed to Heaven hundreds of years prior, came to earth to talk to Jesus about His approaching "decease," which is translated from the Greek *exodos*, which literally means "exit" or "departure."[3] They were telling Jesus that He was leaving earth soon, so they knew His future. And again, from Hebrews 12:1, we are surrounded by a great cloud of witnesses. This verse in context lets us know that we have an accountability to our onlooking family in Christ to not walk in sin but to run the good race in front of us.

Enter another incredible story tied to the dream Sammi had years ago when our son first left for Heaven. My awe for how the Spirit segues one scene into another will never grow old. I can't wait to one day sit at Jesus' feet and see how He does it all.

Gone Fishing: Part 3

"Hello, Sarah. Are you sitting down?" That's how Jenny began her phone call to tell me about the amazing visit by her son, Kevin, to his close friend and her baby.

Let me give a little history. Jenny's son, Kevin, went to Heaven in 2011. At the time he was serving in Afghanistan and had only recently rededicated his life to Christ. After years of praying him back into a walk with Jesus, Jenny received this life-giving letter dated May 11, the day before he went to Heaven.

> A friend of mine invited me to church on base. After the first time I attended a service, I sat there wondering where I had been. I felt like I was at home. I started going every week. It felt really good to get back into it again and rededicate my life to God! I had just gotten so burned out on it that I'd just set it aside for so long. It's great, you know? I feel like a brand-new person. I know I don't have to deal with all life's struggles by myself anymore and that I am saved. I'll talk to you later! Take care. Love you.

In Jenny's own words:

> Only weeks after giving his life back to Christ, my son was received into eternity. What an amazing gift from the Lord to have in my possession Kevin's testimony written by his own hand, sharing with

his mom how he had come back and the peace he was now living in. A cherished gift.

While on earth, prior to his deployment, Kevin spent a lot of time with a couple. These close friends had a baby boy several months after my son went to Heaven, and they named him Kevin. What a precious honor for my mom's heart. I had mailed your book *Have Heart* to the couple months back because I knew they needed to hear the truth of Heaven and to know more about what Kevin's eternal life was looking like. Somewhere within the below time frame, the young mother had the thought that she needed to pick that book up again.

The wife called me one night and said she wanted to tell me something but hoped I would not be mad at her. She said that she was in the living room on the couch with her baby when he became fussy. He was crying and inconsolable. She decided to get up and go to the baby's room and rock him for a while to try and comfort him. She said the baby suddenly stopped crying and was looking toward the door. She looked up to see what he was looking at, and my son was standing in the doorway. He "initially had a sad facial expression," but then she felt that he "looked joyful and content" and had an expression that told her "I'm okay and I have the answers." She got up to go toward him, but he was gone as quickly as he appeared.

She was afraid I would be mad that he visited her and not me. I told her I was so happy that he visited her and that she called to tell me about it. We discussed what she thought he was trying to tell her or the message he wanted her to get. She was not sure but wondered if he was sad that he was not here on earth with us anymore, but the joy and contentment he had when his expression changed did not really say that. As Kevin's mom and a follower of Christ, I knew perfectly well that my son was absolutely happy living in Heaven and did not have any sadness or want to come and live back here on earth. But she was confused. I asked her if she had read the book *Have Heart*. She told me she had not read it yet, but it had been on her mind. I asked her to please read it through and to call me back when she finished.

A few weeks later she called. She was excited to tell me that she now felt like she knew why he visited her and the message he had for her. She told me that she had gotten to a place in the book about the Muslim man's dream, and it all became clear. In her own life she was done with God and religion. *Done.* She said that just like Sammi, she didn't know God and realized that Kevin's sad expression was because she wasn't going to Heaven. She felt like he initially looked sad because he wanted *her* to know Jesus and His love for her and to go to Heaven at the end of her earthly life. She

felt he then looked different because he wanted her
to know the peace and joy in his soul that he now
has in Heaven.

As she was telling me this, I was driving home
and it was raining. I looked up and a double rainbow had formed in the sky. I pulled up a hill, and
the rainbow was ending at my house. I smiled as I
knew that Father God, my son, and the Heavens
were telling me the joy they had in her revelation.

Jenny and I both realize the joy unspeakable of knowing that
our boys are a part of the ongoing eternal story. Through dreams,
the Lord allowed Josiah to fish for Sammi until he was caught. Then
the Lord used Sammi's dream and a holy visitation from a saint in
Heaven to catch yet another soul. The Lord can break through all
our experiences to show His ability to seek and save the lost. He is
anointed for this! He has the chops.

Jesus has defeated death, and in certain situations, He finds it necessary to blow our minds with an unexpected turn of events. This
reminds me of Martha at the tomb of Lazarus in John 11:39–44.

Jesus said, "Take away the stone."

Martha, the sister of him who was dead, said
to Him, "Lord, by this time there is a stench, for he
has been dead four days."

Jesus said to her, "Did I not say to you that if you would believe you would see the glory of God?" Then they took away the stone from the place where the dead man was lying. And Jesus lifted up His eyes and said, "Father, I thank You that You have heard Me. And I know that You always hear Me, but because of the people who are standing by I said this, that they may believe that You sent Me." Now when He had said these things, He cried with a loud voice, "Lazarus, come forth!" And he who had died came out bound hand and foot with graveclothes, and his face was wrapped with a cloth. Jesus said to them, "Loose him, and let him go."

Martha, it seems, was thinking, *No, no, Jesus! Don't do that! My brother has been dead for four days. Don't roll that stone away, please.* I don't think it would be reaching to assume she had great anxiety over Jesus' request. But Jesus was getting ready to shatter Martha's mind with the wonder of His supernatural power. Her grief was on the brink of destruction.

The stone was a wedge between the living and the dead. Jesus spoke the word and that wedge was removed. If at His word the people gathering removed that stone, then it is not a reach to imagine Christ commanding the veil to be pulled back for the furtherance of His Kingdom.

Second Kings holds an example of God supernaturally pulling back the veil:

So [Elisha] answered, "Do not fear, for those who are with us are more than those who are with them." And Elisha prayed, and said, "LORD, I pray, open his eyes that he may see." Then the LORD opened the eyes of the young man, and he saw. And behold, the mountain was full of horses and chariots of fire all around Elisha. So when the Syrians came down to him, Elisha prayed to the LORD, and said, "Strike this people, I pray, with blindness." And He struck them with blindness according to the word of Elisha. (6:16–18)

You can be certain the young man with Elisha, who had been walking in fear, was now operating in emboldened faith. He needed to know they were not alone in this holy battle, and God benevolently made it clear. The Lord can pull back the veil and give humanity the ability to see with spiritual eyes when and if He deems it essential in the moment. Likewise, He can blind others from seeing anything, all for the furtherance of His Kingdom. He makes it clear in the Word that He is not about doing any of these supernatural exploits for show. These scenes are always created to capture the lost or encourage saints along their way, just as we see in the above story.

Let's look at a New Testament passage that will tie a few things together for us:

And Jesus came and spoke to [the eleven disciples], saying, *"All authority has been given to Me in heaven and on earth. Go therefore and make disciples of*

all the nations, baptizing them in the name of
the Father and of the Son and of the Holy Spirit,
teaching them to observe all things that I have commanded you; and lo, I am with you always, even to
the end of the age." Amen. (Matt. 28:18–20)

Remember, these words were spoken over the followers of Jesus
after His resurrection. Imagine the impact on the crowd and the
encouragement they received from Jesus walking the earth for forty
days after being resurrected from the dead. Their hopes had been
obliterated at the cross as their Messiah was brutally murdered, and
now they were experiencing the wonder of seeing Him alive again.
You'd better believe they knew He had all authority; they had seen
Him conquer death! Been there, done that!

Now that we have a fuller understanding of the community of
saints in Heaven and through the Word a better grasp on His power,
we can see the Great Commission with a fresh perspective. The body
of Christ—on earth *and* in Heaven—works together, each taking
his or her own part in the "fishing." Some plant, others harvest, but
God brings the growth (see 1 Cor. 3:6).

Hawaii, Thanksgiving 2012

In October 2012, I had a prophetic dream with Josiah that would
work to establish an absolute in my heart concerning eternal life.
Jesus picked me up and gave me a pass to skip so many of the other
steps in grief that many walk through. Not because I am at all special but because I simply believed! There was no going back; I was
changed.

This detailed dream would prove to this mom what the Word clearly says, "that mortality may be swallowed up by life" (2 Cor. 5:4). Our loved ones are proud of us when we agree with Christ. Our loved ones want us living in the reality that they are alive. That they are given a degree of knowledge about our lives whether seen by their own eyes or relayed by the Spirit. At times they are cast into the holy script, filled with sets and detail the Lord has created with His master-creator mind.

In my dream, I had the perspective of standing from behind and watching. Our entire family sat together on what seemed to be a garden wall, with our legs dangling, looking out into a beautiful tropical yard with a rectangular pool. It was a location I had never seen before in real life. To my left sat a young Josiah; the rest of the family sat on my right. Josiah appeared to be about four, adorable and at that stage of life where every little boy has a crush on his mom.

Josiah leaned up and gave me several kisses on my left cheek, his love for me on overload. Then he looked into my eyes and said, "Mom, you *know* that I'm mature, and you *know* that I'm alive in Heaven!" My response was, "Yes, buddy, I know that you are a mature man of God and that you are fully alive in Heaven."

The next morning, as I described the dream to my husband, I wept. My heart was broken, and I was barely able to eke out the words. As I shared about precious little Josiah, my heart ached to see him again. I told Steve that I didn't know what the Lord was saying, but I was certain this lucid dream was by His own hand. Steve immediately interpreted the dream for me, at least in part. He said the Lord was saying that although Josiah is entirely mature, spiritually speaking, the Father wanted me to know that Josiah loves me with as much passion as he had as a little boy. My tears just ran and ran. What a treasure to receive encouragement that Josiah is still in love with his mom.

When Josiah had spoken those words, he'd been very assertive, and he'd put an emphasis on the word *know* both times it was used. I sensed in the dream that he was so proud of me that I was getting it. It was like, "Go get 'em, Mom!" I was receiving all the truth the Lord was offering in the Word through this journey of grief and claiming it as my own, and my boy knew it.

So what about our surroundings? What with the garden and pool? Not long after the dream, Steve and I both felt an idea stirring in our hearts. Thanksgiving was only two weeks away, and we wanted to get away with the kids. We prayed and asked the Lord what He thought would be good for us. Some dear friends of ours owned a house on the island of Maui and had offered it to us many times in the past. In a moment, we knew that was the answer! We made a quick phone call, and as the Lord would have it, the house was available.

I remember the joy and anticipation of this family vacation. We had come up with a family motto many months earlier—"Always 6, Never 5"—which meant that we are forever a family of six. Siah is still a part of our family even though he is now living in Heaven. So off we went on our Hawaiian adventure.

We arrived at our vacation home close to sunset—a beautiful place full of the aloha spirit, as any Hawaiian would say. As we walked into the house, I peered out the sliding glass door. There was a deep deck, and from the threshold I couldn't immediately see the steps down. As I continued to look out, my jaw dropped.

The view from the deck was of a beautiful tropical landscape with a rectangular pool. *This was the spot from my dream!*

"This is the spot!" I all but shouted. "This is the spot! How did You do that, Lord?" He had provided an incredible dream to give credibility to the truth He'd been reiterating about Heaven and the saints being alive. *Then* He'd gone the extra mile to prove He knew where we would be traveling and, by the Holy Spirit, had stirred us toward making our extravagant and spontaneous Thanksgiving plans in the first place.

The Lord was saying so many things in the dream. If you haven't connected the dots quite yet, Josiah knew we were heading to Hawaii, and as a matter to ponder, I believe he was, to whatever degree, there with us—the communion of the saints and togetherness—although through the veil. I don't know exactly how to convey it, but just with us.

Later that week, as our family strolled through Lahaina, we came across an art gallery that we had visited on a previous trip. We absolutely loved the art, and the artist happened to be in the shop that day. Curiously enough, he asked how many were in our family. We exchanged knowing glances, and someone answered, "Six." He said, "I ask because people will frequently ask me to paint their families into the paintings that I have done to make them more personal. With that, he added our entire family to a painting—our beautiful four children, including Josiah, my hubby, and me. The artist signed the back of the painting with our family motto: "Always 6, Never 5."

What a divine script! The Lord will go far and beyond to heal our broken hearts because He is called and anointed like no other. When He heals, He heals to the utmost.

> Seeing that we have a great High Priest who has passed through the heavens, Jesus the Son of God, let us hold fast our confession. For we do not have a High Priest who cannot sympathize with our weaknesses, but was in all points tempted as we are, yet without sin. Let us therefore come boldly to the throne of grace, that we may obtain mercy and find grace to help in time of need. (Heb. 4:14–16)

Allow yourself permission to believe Him fully at His word. Perhaps like me, you too will be able to skip some painful steps in your journey for having fully believed.

Maybe, as you walk through your own sorrow, you are being stretched beyond your comfort zone with these stories. I want to gently urge you to please take it up with your amazing God.

But first, hear the apostle Paul, as he wrote to the church in Corinth:

> It is doubtless not profitable for me to boast. I will come to visions and revelations of the Lord: I know a man in Christ who fourteen years ago— whether in the body I do not know, or whether out of the body I do not know, God knows—such

a one was caught up to the third heaven. And I know such a man—whether in the body or out of the body I do not know, God knows—how he was caught up into Paradise and heard inexpressible words, which it is not lawful for a man to utter. Of such a one I will boast; yet of myself I will not boast, except in my infirmities. For though I might desire to boast, I will not be a fool; for I will speak the truth. But I refrain, lest anyone should think of me above what he sees me to be or hears from me. (2 Cor. 12:1–6)

I also bring you John the Revelator:

After these things I looked, and behold, a door standing open in heaven. And the first voice which I heard was like a trumpet speaking with me, saying, "Come up here, and I will show you things which must take place after this." (Rev. 4:1)

My heart behind sharing all this is to quell fires of unbelief or divisiveness. Please, I pray, go to the Lord with your sorrow. Possibly you've not understood how truly extravagant He is. He will leave the ninety-nine to go after the one (see Luke 15:4–7). Be honest. Can you find fault in Him for reaching a wounded Muslim via supernatural dreams that led him to receive Jesus as his Savior? I'm so grateful the Lord doesn't stop at our human limits but far exceeds them all.

Reflection

"Mom, you *know* I'm alive in Heaven!"

Sisters, isn't the possibility of bringing joy to Heaven beautiful? Just as the heavenly hosts rejoice to see one sinner saved (see Luke 15:7), surely, they must love to see fellow saints on earth act and speak the reality of eternal life in Heaven.

What does your language look like? Jot down a few terms you've used that didn't line up with the truth of the Word. Then write truth! Doesn't that make a difference?

chapter 11

waves of reason

Deep calls unto deep at the noise of Your waterfalls;
all Your waves and billows have gone over me.
The LORD will command His lovingkindness in the daytime,
and in the night His song shall be with me—
a prayer to the God of my life.

Psalm 42:7–8

The Lord has a unique way of reasoning His people into growth and change. His means of compelling us forward are wildly creative and seldom redundant. You see, He knows our very frame and language. He will repeat, jump up and down, wave a flag, or shout it from the rooftop—all in His loving effort to get us up and moving in the right direction (or up and engaging in conversation with Him).

In January 2018, I found myself sitting on my bed with Bible study notes strewn all over the duvet. The following morning, I was to teach on hearing God's voice of reason and how to identify when He speaks. I was reasoning with the Lord on the many ways He speaks and wondering how in the world I was going to cover it all in one forty-minute teaching.

I asked Him to edit and show me what specifically I needed to cover to communicate His heart and Word with clarity. In just moments, I heard a still, small voice say, "Sometimes this way, sometimes that." I knew those words! They were familiar to me, as I have read them—or words like them—many times.

Have you ever heard specific words or phrases repeating in your mind? It may be once a week or once a year, but still—it's there. Possibly the words aren't even familiar, but they're there in your mind. When that happens, I encourage you to open your Bible and do a word search to see if it's God speaking to you. Take note: if you find yourself suddenly remembering or thinking on a specific verse (or simply a few words pulled from a verse), *go with it!* He is saying something you're not gonna want to miss.

When God spoke, "Sometimes this way, sometimes that," He was referencing Job 33:14–16, which says, "For God may speak in one way, or in another, yet man does not perceive it. In a dream, in a vision of the night, when deep sleep falls upon men, while slumbering on their beds, then He opens the ears of men, and seals their instruction."

I would encourage you to read the book of Job, or at minimum, chapter 33. The words above were spoken by an unexpected voice of reason, a young man named Elihu, whose name translates as "he is my God himself."[1] In this case, I am certain that Job and his friends were not prepared to hear from such a young lad. Certainly, the Lord would use a much older and wiser man of God to confront their intellect, right? Nope, the Spirit of God was bursting in this Elihu. He knew the answer to their dilemma, and in the appointed moment, he spoke.

Like Job and his friends, we also need to be cognizant of the reality that God speaks often to us and in any way He chooses. The Lord may use someone or something to deliver His message that may offend our thinking minds, but again—we don't want to miss it. Imagine if Job and his friends had ignored the wisdom of Elihu. Imagine if all the dreams in the Bible had been hastily ignored and never recorded for our reading. What a loss it would be to us and particularly to those the Master and Creator had designed them for. Our job is to pay attention, testing everything against the Word to make sure we're not entertaining vain imaginations.

> His means of compelling us
> forward are wildly creative
> and seldom redundant.

So, while I sat among my sea of teaching notes, I asked the Lord if He might give me a word picture to drive His point home with the ladies—a visual they might remember and apply the next time there was a sense that He may be speaking and inviting them to reason with Him. To be true, seldom does this happen in my life, but in this case, I immediately heard, "It's like riding a wave."

At the speed of God, I knew His intent! It was an analogy that resonated to my core. I was raised on the West Coast and spent all my summers in Laguna Beach. Throughout my childhood, I'd often be found out in the water with a raft, ready to catch the next wave. Imagine for a minute that you're out in the water on your own raft.

Your heart is pounding, and as the waves swell and approach, you have to decide, *Am I going to paddle hard to catch this or pull back and resist?*

Job 33:29–33 says:

> Behold, God works all these things,
> Twice, in fact, three times with a man,
> To bring back his soul from the Pit,
> That he may be enlightened with the light of life.
>
> Give ear, Job, listen to me;
> Hold your peace, and I will speak.
> If you have anything to say, answer me;
> Speak, for I desire to justify you.
> If not, listen to me;
> Hold your peace, and I will teach you wisdom.

Just as in Job, God speaks, the wave is offered, but much of the time we miss it; that is, we do not perceive it. While waiting to catch a wave, there will be times of disappointment. There will be moments of knowing, *Man, I missed it! Look at that wave! That was for me, and I missed it.*

But because of God's grace, He presents yet another, and another—two, three times, or more—until we perceive His voice and agree to catch the wave. Fear not: If you've missed Him in times past, He is faithful to offer another wave. Just be patient and wait! He longs to enlighten us with His wisdom.

Like waves, God's messages are presented to us as He speaks. Sometimes swells slip by us, whether because we're just too lazy or because we don't make an effort to ride out the reasoning. Other times, we see, or rather hear, the swell of His voice. We catch the wave but choose to pull out prematurely. And then there are swells that are just flat-out too scary, and we choose not to ride them at all.

Might I suggest what a scary wave might look like in the form of a challenging word? How about *forgive, sacrifice,* or *repent*? Maybe your daunting wave sounds like mine: *It's time for you to move from the home you've built tender memories in for the past fifteen years. The home your kids spent their school years in. The home in which your son who is now in Heaven lived his last years on earth.*

Some may reject a ride like that. Just too tender ... too many wounds ... so much sorrow. But what opportunity, what adventure, what healing might we miss by choosing to simply float instead of ride?

The decision to ride a wave like that depends on trusting our Father's character and believing He is good. We know by both experiential knowledge and His Word that He is good, but do we trust Him enough in the deep waters to ride the waves, even the challenging ones?

Spiritually speaking, if you stay in the shallow, knee-high waters, the reasoning, the conversation, or the ride may at times be really easy, but "really easy" over and over does not bring growth. If you avoid the daunting waves that push you beyond your own strength and understanding, you'll never receive the healing God will meet you with at shore, nor will your trust in Christ increase. If you choose not to ride, you may find yourself spiritually stuck, and you may not reach the shore at all.

However, if you trust Him, engage with His voice, and ride the wave, you'll find yourself safe at shore, picking up that raft and running right back into the water for another ride.

Thank You, Jesus, for gently teaching us to hear and trust Your voice close to shore before leading us to deeper waters. May we trust You in the tender, scary places that we've chosen in times past to resist. May we all ride Your waves of reason and ultimately make it all the way to shore.

Reflection

Earlier in the chapter, I said that when God speaks to us, it is like waves that offer themselves to us, in hope that we will catch them and ride them. What "waves" do you sense He has offered you—but you never caught them? What may you have missed? Are you sensing any new waves coming your way? Are you willing to catch the next wave, trusting your Father as you ride it out?

Lord, we can't bear to miss a thing. Please illuminate us with the light of life. In Jesus, name.

chapter 12

waves of change

How shall we escape if we neglect so great a salvation,
which at the first began to be spoken by the Lord, and was
confirmed to us by those who heard Him, God also bearing
witness both with **signs and wonders**, *with* **various miracles**,
and gifts of the Holy Spirit, according to His own will?"

Hebrews 2:3–4

The morning after God gave me the "waves of reason" analogy, I received a phone call from Josiah's friend Lucy. (Yes, the same Lucy who dreamed of Josiah becoming an eagle back in chapter 7.) She has become a close friend of ours since he left for Heaven. The Lord has cinched my heart with hers as we have walked out this great grief together. God speaks to Lucy with much clarity through dreams, and anytime I hear from her, I *know* she'll have something incredible and heavenly to share. The Lord has used her time and time again to ignite my heart when the fire was dimming a bit.

I was excited to see her name show up on my caller ID, but I knew I had no time for a lengthy conversation, as I was walking out the door for church to teach the Word on "Reasoning through the

Waves." Nonetheless, I answered the phone because … well, it was Lucy!

"Hey, Lucy—what's up?"

"I had a dream with Josiah last night, and I had to call and tell you about it." From the familiar tone of her voice, I just knew she had something profound to share. Excitedly I replied, "Oh, Lucy, I'm heading out the door for Bible study and don't have time to talk. I'll call you immediately after study, okay?" I remember thinking, *I wonder if her dream would have spoken toward my teaching today.*

As soon as Bible study ended, I glanced at my phone and there it was—a portion of the dream Lucy had texted while I was teaching. I'd completely forgotten about the early morning call, but here is what she texted:

> In my dream, I asked Josiah, "How is every-thing going?" I remember what he said!! He said, "Everything is good. I am watching the waves roll in," and he showed me a video he had captured somehow of waves rolling across the screen like a very subtle tsunami. Like, not huge waves.
>
> He was wearing a blue, black, and white-striped jersey. Looked like a soccer jersey to me. Ha ha. And his hair, Sarah, was *huge*! The street was icy, and he guided me down the street like ice skat-ing. I remember looking at my shoes and laughing. But get this—we were on your property, but it was like a huge farm. I've had a similar dream with him on that same property you guys owned.

I was so excited about the Lord's kindness. He had allowed Josiah to show up in a friend's dream—a friend who would then text me to confirm that the word He had given me about riding a wave really was from *Him*! The truth that God speaks to us and that we can actually hear Him will never grow old. John 10:27 says, "My sheep hear my voice, and I know them, and they follow me" (ESV). I love how God ties things together to confirm His word and speaks in such a way that no one but *He* could ever get the credit.

There is more to Lucy's dream that is so very significant. She wrote this insight:

> The waves appeared on an enormous movie screen. The vantage point was unusual, though. It was as if the footage was shot out at sea and the waves were moving toward a shoreline so distant it couldn't be seen. Wave after wave in cadence was moving toward earth's shoreline. Wouldn't that make it so much more tempting to pull out and turn back simply because of the unknown?

That part about the gigantic movie screen caught my attention, because over the years, I've experienced in my own dreams and the dreams of others that anytime a screen, photo, or transparency appears in the dream, it usually speaks to the veil between Heaven and earth. God is trying to tell us that the veil is not as thick or opaque as we often suspect.

Yes, the saints and angels are outside our means of measuring time, but God often uses them in dreams. He has proven in His

Word that He can give the heavenly hosts and saints a knowing or a seeing into future events of life here on earth when He chooses.

Remember Elijah and Moses at the Mount of Transfiguration, sharing with Jesus about His nearing departure from earth (see Matt. 17:1–8)? This is an amazing account, mentioned previously in chapter 10 of this book, of heavenly saints appearing not just in a dream but visibly on earth! They knew Jesus would be leaving the earth soon. Referring to Elijah and Moses, Luke 9:31 says they "appeared in glory and spoke of His decease [or, exit from earth] which He was about to accomplish at Jerusalem." It is not lost on me that although Moses and Elijah had been living in Heaven for hundreds of years, they were aware of future events concerning Jesus. At God's ordained moment, they passed through the veil to discuss these approaching events with their King.

God sent two patriarchs of the faith back to earth to deliver a timely and, I'm certain, difficult word. Jesus, knowing of His impending death, must have felt some degree of strength and courage after being reunited with friends who could stand and remind Him of the victory coming and send word from His heavenly Home. I imagine them bringing word of saints who were awaiting His heavenly return and news that they were all praying and interceding for the King as His self-sacrifice approached. How reassuring in His most trying moments! Christ would soon be there with them again—returning to take His rightful place in His Kingdom after defeating death, hell, and the grave (see Rev. 1:17b–18).

You see, Lucy's dream is one of many we have been given with a fellow believer in Heaven participating. The impact of these God dreams reaches to our very souls. To think our good God would script a friend, saint, watcher, or son into a dream—especially one that speaks prophetically into our future—is beyond amazing.

A Holy Car Wash

One year after Josiah left for Heaven, our daughter Heather did a college semester abroad in Seville, Spain, to study Spanish. My sister-in-law Marianne and I took advantage of the opportunity to travel to Europe and visit our precious Heather. While in Seville, I had the most incredible dream.

In the dream, I was entering a drive-through car wash. As I pulled up, I saw a friend named Karen, who had left for Heaven just months earlier. I rolled down the window and was yelling, "Karen, Karen!" She calmly said, "Tell Gigi to have a blowout New Year, and tell Jeff to pick up and embrace Siegfried."

I barely heard her last words before rolling up the window. Beside me, in the passenger seat, was a Spanish woman I had seen in a shop the day before. "That's my friend Karen!" I told her. "Do you understand? She lives in Heaven!"

Wow! The next morning, I shared the dream with Heather and Marianne. I knew in my gut that I must go back to the shop that day. *If* by chance the woman from my dream was there, I needed to assure her that Heaven is real and that followers of Christ are alive in Heaven, because in the dream that's what I was trying to convince her of. This was my only chance, as we would be flying home the very next day. I didn't want to risk missing being obedient to God's compelling.

We walked through Seville, found the little shop once again, and—lo and behold—in a chair against the wall sat this same woman! She didn't work there but was the owner's friend and just happened to be visiting again. She spoke no English, but I speak Spanish relatively well and felt confident that I could communicate in her language all God had for me to share. I asked if she could come sit outside on a bench with me. I told her, "Last night, I had a dream, and the Lord wants me to tell you that Heaven is real and that your family and friends who have passed away who trusted in Jesus for salvation are indeed alive!"

She began to cry and told me she'd been praying and asking the Lord if they were really alive. I explained Hebrews 12:1 and how we are surrounded by a cloud of witnesses. She was so touched that Jesus would answer her prayers by giving a dream to an American woman, who would then search her out and assure her of Heaven's reality. I was so honored that He would include me to see to the needs of His sweet daughter who was praying from another part of the world.

That part of the story was incredible enough, but wait—there's more! I still had to return home and deliver Karen's messages to Gigi and Jeff. When I arrived, I continued to pray about the two words Karen had given me. One for my sister-in-law Gigi and the other for Karen's widowed husband, Jeff. I prayed for weeks about these words to seek confirmation. Both words were so curious, as if we were to solve some sort of riddle. Who was Siegfried? I'd assumed they had a dog by that name, and looking back, I just laugh. Finally, at God's prompting, I looked up the meaning of the name, never imagining that it would have any significance—and boy, was I shocked. *Siegfried* means "victorious peace"! Karen was conveying that Jeff needed to pick up and embrace victorious peace.

I called Jeff soon after the revelation of this word and very gently conveyed the message. Jeff was kind, but it was apparent that he was not going to pick this up—even if the word was coming straight from his wife alive in Heaven. "Victory in Jesus, Jeff! Karen is alive in the Kingdom, and you need to walk in this truth. Walk in 'victorious peace,' and you will receive His rest!" Sadly, Jeff lived out his days stumbling in his faith, and his ministry was never the same.

Upon calling my dear sister-in-law Gigi, I told her about my dream and Karen conveying the message to have a blowout New Year. Gigi received it and began to pray. A few hours later, Gigi texted, saying she had looked up the definition of *blowout* and that it meant an easy or one-sided victory. She said, "I know what my victory would be: my mom receiving Jesus this year!" I was so excited because it was evident that the Lord had spoken to Gigi—and she received it! And by the end of that very year, a month before her ninetieth birthday, Gigi's mother received Jesus as her Savior. Within months, she slipped away into eternity. Now, *that* is a blowout year indeed!

Finally, concerning the dream, what about the car? The car wash? I have prayed about this much, and it seems clear to me that the car conveyed that this dear Spanish woman and I were in this together—that we were in Christ (the car) experiencing a divine appointment. The car was being pulled by a mechanism, and the movement was out of my control—reminiscent of the Holy Spirit. The car wash felt to me like His way of washing over us both with a lavish experience, and on the other side of that was the reality of the world. Like, *Okay, here we go!* I take such comfort and joy from these dreams—not just for our sakes, but imagining how sweet it is from Heaven's perspective is a double blessing!

> Heaven has swung low many
> times in different, outstanding,
> creative ways—ways far
> beyond what my human mind
> could ever come up with.

I'm betting Karen and Josiah love when Creator God scripts a dream in which they are cast. Knowing my son well, I can just hear him react to the opportunity. "Oh man, I can't wait to see Lucy's reaction! This is going to be awesome! And when she tells Mom? She's gonna flip!" I bet this is the same for any one of the watchers or holy ones who are called to participate. What a beautiful bridge between Heaven and earth.

I am so incredibly thankful to our Father God for the time He has spent caring for our family and all of Josiah's community he left here on earth. Heaven has swung low many times in different, outstanding, creative ways—ways far beyond what my human mind could ever come up with.

A Wave of Reason: The Big Move

As the Lord would have it, simultaneously with this word on reasoning, He had begun to speak to me about moving out of our home. He spoke to me through a unique process—unexpected emotion—that proved Him sovereign. The Spirit deposited the thought into my mind and made my heart glad (even excited) over the possibility. The first time I felt this, I disregarded the wave, or the idea, because you see, we were never going to move from that home. It wasn't even remotely in our hearts. We'd talked about possibly building a small getaway along the river, but we never entertained the idea of moving to another residence.

The Lord says in Job 33:29–30 that He will say something twice and even three times, and that's just what He did. I had this same sense or experience several times over a period of weeks. However, I dared not mention it to a soul until I was certain it was the Lord, as I did not want to speak the words carelessly. Speaking out too soon about something as tender as this, and the possibility of moving forward outside of His perfect will, could mean enormous sorrow and anxiety. Our very hearts were on the line if in fact this was not His idea.

At last, I realized these waves of emotion, if you will, were actually the Lord presenting a ride. I felt an unexplained anticipation about the possibilities. The God-given excitement gave me the push to paddle with the swell and ride. Where would all of this lead? I prayed, "God, I need to trust You. You are good and have purpose far beyond my understanding. This looks and feels like You, to pose an idea so far from anything I've ever thought of, so it is time to test the waters."

I started by very cautiously mentioning the idea of moving to my husband. "Roo [my nickname for him], I've been sitting on something for a few weeks now. It is so random, and honestly, I'm a bit nervous to even speak it out. I've had this crazy idea of moving percolating in my heart. Like, I even have a degree of excitement and anticipation over the possibility, which is perplexing! It scares me for all the obvious reasons, but I can't deny that it feels like it's God because it's that out of the box."

After talking through it all, it was obvious that the Lord had also been preparing his heart for the possibility. Steve was on board, and we were ready to ride this out together, seeking God's divine direction at every turn. We wondered, *Why? Where? How?* We agreed that our divine confirmation, our "fleece" (see Judg. 6:36–40), would come through our kids. This would be our way of setting up the idea to possibly be shut down. Once we brought them in and saw where their hearts were, we'd have a clearer picture. For our kids to agree with the prospect of moving would be like tossing a fleece into water and asking God to completely wring it dry to prove His will.

You see, we'd been in this location for fourteen years and had lived a lot of life there. We are not the type who move a lot, so we had spent many years building memories in our home. My own childhood was lived out in only one home, surrounded by cattle and open spaces. Likewise, God's will for our family has been to plant and settle us for long seasons of time. This house especially held a tender place because it was the last earthly home we shared with Josiah.

This was major! How would moving impact our memories of Siah? How would we handle his belongings in a new house? These were questions that needed to be handled with intention. A move is a big deal, and as followers of Christ, we must come to Him honestly about every aspect of all things. For a grieving family, it was even more important for us to be aware of possible pitfalls and sensitively seek God's direction.

After all, Jesus had given me such distinct direction when Josiah had left for Heaven. I told Him I'd perish if He didn't instruct me in every step. I dared not approach anything without consulting Him first. This tightness to the Master had given me my life's breath over the past ten years as He has kept me from making decisions that could have made this journey even more precarious.

Falling out of step with the Lord's will can always be redeemed, but leaning into Him at every step holds the benefit of knowing He is guiding us through tender situations that can be doable, even enjoyable, on this side of the veil. He can turn our mourning into dancing (see Ps. 30:11)!

When a family has experienced great grief, it is important to weigh all hearts and lean on God for decisions and timing—at least this is how the Lord has tutored us. Although we don't depend on our kids making decisions for us, there are times like this when it is beneficial to hear their opinions, knowing they are mature enough in Christ to hear His voice even in sacred places.

> When a family has experienced
> great grief, it is important to
> weigh all hearts and lean on
> God for decision and timing.

The issues surrounding a potential move were tough waves to reason through, but with His divine help, we walked forward in great hope. Apart from His reassurance and direction, we would never have made so great a decision, one with the potential to shatter our hearts.

So, one Sunday at a family gathering, we broached the subject of moving with our kids. We were surprised to learn that God had already been preparing their hearts as well. It was apparent that both Heather and Cody had thought of this before. They'd been concerned for us and our privacy.

You see, the Lord had prompted us fifteen years prior to purchase land right beside the church my husband pastored. When Steve first mentioned purchasing the land and building a home, I was adamantly opposed. I told him, "There is no way I am going to live next door to the church and risk our family losing all sense of normalcy!" Before going to bed that night, he asked me to pray about it for twenty-four hours. Ugh. I'd hoped he'd already forgotten, but I reluctantly agreed.

Jesus came in swiftly, and by morning, He had spoken: "What you see as a curse, I mean as a blessing!" You cannot make this stuff up. Literally, God pulled down all my fears with this word. He knew all my concerns about the location, and with this answer He shattered them all. Even though the land was so close to the church, He assured me that we would be nearly invisible to the crowd.

I must add this, because God's provision is so crazy: After agreeing with the Lord and my husband on this enormous decision, the next question was how in the world we could afford to purchase the land. We prayed for direction, and by the end of the same week, we received an inheritance check. This money had sat in probate for nine years. It was money from my aunt Trudy, who had gone to Heaven years earlier. That check was a "divine delay," as a friend of mine would say. The King of Glory kept it at bay until *the* right moment. That gift paid for all but $1,000 of the five acres.

All this said, the church had grown to such a degree over the fifteen years since we had purchased the property that its 175-acre campus practically enveloped our home. We had become a single-family residence surrounded by church traffic and school buildings. It was glorious, but we felt it was time to go. This was why Heather and Cody were concerned for us. They were both married, were out of the house, and had a different perspective.

There was still a conversation we needed to have with our youngest child, our daughter Destiny. She still lived at home with us, so the fleece felt like even more of a risk. As I unfolded to her the direction we were sensing, she said, "If you'd have mentioned this just a few weeks ago, I think I'd have been mad, but today it feels right." We were amazed how God spoke to our hearts in His timing to align our minds with His will.

With the momentous decision made, we prayed for direction—I mean, literal direction! "Where, Lord? North? South? East? West?" We felt Him dangling a Holy Ghost carrot, leading us to look south of our current location.

My conversations with God went something like this: "Father, we have caught this wave, and I need to trust You more with where it leads! To a development? A renovation? A new build? Father, I've grown accustomed to having some land, and yet You know what's best. You can change my heart, and I can adapt to wherever You lead." The ride at times felt a bit scary, but because I know God's nature and His desire for the good of His children, I trusted Him. I believe these opportunities of risk and trust will bear much fruit when followed.

Within a few weeks, we found ourselves leading our annual pilgrimage in Israel. While in Jerusalem, we enjoyed visiting with some dear friends who live in the area. As we finished our dinner, my friend Alis had one last thing to mention before we said our goodbyes: "This morning I was praying for you, and the Lord gave me a vision of you both."

"Really? What was it, Alis?" I questioned.

"Well, you were both riding a wave. You came closer and closer together until you were both riding on the same board." (Get it? Both *on board*?!)

Steve and I just looked at each other. *No way! God, You are amazing! You didn't have to do it, but You went out of Your way to make sure we both received a reminder that this move was You!*

Upon hearing this third witness, I began to really soak in what we were stepping into. I was both excited and concerned at the same time. So I reasoned with God again: "Father, You are going to have to help me with packing up Josiah's room. How do I process this?"

The idea of removing all his things felt too heavy and horribly sad. You see, we'd not changed a thing in Josiah's room since he went to Heaven. The Lord instructed us to leave everything as it was and to live in the knowing that Siah is alive! He simply left his earthly home and room and is now living in another country, a new city, "whose builder and maker is God" (Heb. 11:10).

We'd heard of other grieving families who had shut rooms off— as if they were forbidden or too sullen to even step into. But for us, it was as if Jesus had told us, "Not you. Open those doors. Open those shades. Let the light shine in, even through many grievous tears. Your Josiah lives in the Homeland; he simply doesn't need this room any longer."

So when Siah first left, we were very intentional about leaving the door open to his room. We didn't shut it off, only to be entered in a moment of anguish to languish. His room wasn't some strange idolatrous shrine. No, the door was open, and it brought life to our souls and to friends and family.

Sacred though the room may be to some, it was a space our son enjoyed, laughed in, and slept in. We knew neither God nor Josiah would want it shut off as if to forget all the fun and joy that happened in that space. God said to open the doors, and that is just what we did. I am certain that Josiah, from the cloud of witnesses, took joy in seeing his family moving forward in life—not glorifying death. Again, we did this at God's instruction, contrary to culture, and it was good and right for the Berger family.

So the daunting thought of not having Josiah's room any longer made my eyes tear up and my stomach ache many a time. While I knelt in prayer one day, reasoning through tears with the Lord, I poured out my concern about how desperately I would need His help. Then I heard His still, small voice: "Sarah, what is the most precious thing you own of Josiah's?"

I immediately knew it was his Jeep. I pondered before answering, "Yes, the Jeep." Josiah's old '97 Jeep Wrangler is sentimental to our entire family and to his friends. Steve had surprised him with the Jeep back in '08, when he was a junior at Franklin High School. (You may wonder if this was the vehicle Josiah was driving when the

accident happened. No, it was not. He'd borrowed his sister's car
that night.)

The Jeep is quintessential Siah. When you see it, you just can't
not think of him, donning his latest pair of sunglasses, Angels &
Airwaves or Matisyahu blasting as he cruised downtown Franklin
(otherwise known as DTF). Everyone just loves that old white
Wrangler. Our kids continue to call dibs on it on a beautiful sunny
day. After Siah left for Heaven, his brother, Cody, drove the Jeep for
a season as his school commuter too and gave her the name Gloria.
Lots of fun memories have been made cruisin' in Gloria.

A few years ago, my husband had the sweet idea of fixing her
up just a bit. Some new tires, rims, seats, and a customized license
plate that reads "Siah4x4." One day we drove it into Nashville and
dropped it off at 4 Wheel Parts. When we asked when it might be
finished, they responded August 14. *What?* Josiah's birthday! Sure
enough, the Lord had given us this precious God Nod, and on
Josiah's birthday the family drove off in Siah's Jeep with a kiss from
Heaven.

When we arrived home from Israel, I more seriously searched
the internet for real estate and came across a home that struck me.
I contacted the builder and discovered it had been under contract
but had just fallen through and was now available. Steve and I drove
out to see the house and were immediately smitten. For one, it had a
three-car garage, something we'd never even thought to look for. It
was as if the Lord was saying, "Here ya go! Here's the special spot I
set up just for Josiah's Jeep!" We never even looked at another house.
This was it! Crazy sugar on top: when Lucy was finally able to come
for a visit, she knew this was the house from her dream.

How considerate of God to give this mom the most incredible knowing—when her son in Heaven was already aware this wave was coming. Although Lucy's dream spoke to Josiah's peaceful calm and the eternal perspective the saints and angels in Heaven walk in, this change has been tough at times for those of us here on earth. We've felt the sting of sacrifice, which requires giving up something we hold dear. But if we're able to lay those tough times at the feet of our King in worship, the reward is increased trust in Him.

Within six months, the word, dream, and vision had been fulfilled concerning the move, yet waves continued to present themselves—one powerful tsunami after another. As we know, tsunamis aren't necessarily large in height, but the power with which they move all things in their path is striking. It's a wonder how when God speaks, He moves everything in His path according to His will.

As Your love, in wave after wave
Crashes over me, crashes over me ...

You make me brave
You make me brave
You call me out beyond the shore into the waves ...[1]

Reflection

As your family grieves, pray for wisdom on including other family members in major life decisions when possible—if not to ask for their opinions, at least to allow them to process any potential change.

Romans 12:18 says, "If it is possible, as much as depends on you, live peaceably with all men." "All men" includes family. I realize not all family dynamics will allow for involvement, but when it is possible, include others in the conversation. When Christ is the center, there should be enormous grace for one another.

Father, here we pray for healing and restoration where perhaps conversation didn't happen. We also pray for repentance and reconciliation and sacred do-overs where Jesus wants to touch that wound.

the always available, wonderful counselor

For unto us a Child is born,
Unto us a Son is given;
And the government will be upon His shoulder.
And His name will be called
Wonderful, Counselor, Mighty God,
Everlasting Father, Prince of Peace.

Isaiah 9:6

August 2019 marked the tenth year since our Josiah left for Heaven. To be true, the comfort of Christ has been my constant companion, and His grace has been sufficient through the grief. However, the years 2016–2018 were difficult to a deeper degree and brought with them some unforeseen peril.

Not that the first years weren't tough and filled with thousands of tears, but those more recent years brought more intense sorrow because the issues at hand required a more painstaking look *into* my wound. You see, during those three years we experienced several big changes. Beautiful changes. Happy changes. And yet with any change there comes the sorrow of Josiah not being here and us simply missing his beautiful, ridiculous self.

Along my path, it felt as though this sadness was coupled with a boulder blocking my way and making passage even more difficult. A painful and daunting challenge awaited, and it would be my job to pull out my spiritual crowbar to rid my path of that boulder ... or recoil and allow it to stop me in my tracks. With change comes fear!

The Lord was uncovering stones that needed to be cleared along each step of my journey. In His goodness, He deemed it time to tend to a few chinks in this mom's armor—hidden wounds tucked so deeply into the chambers of my heart that I myself didn't even realize their presence. They had been untended—concealed—until now. It was my turn.

Dream of Deliverance

Until my revelation of the trauma, our lives just simply and beautifully moved forward. Our firstborn, Heather, was wed to her wonderful hubby, Jarrett, in October 2013. Only a year later our son Cody married his beautiful high school sweetheart, Keri. All a blessing! All beautiful additions! But with all the beauty also came the very present knowing that Josiah wasn't here. Not here to cry at his big sis getting married or to dance it up on the reception floor with his younger sister, Destiny. Not here to stand up at the altar with his younger brother, Cody, or watch him grow into the most godly, handsome, kindest husband ever.

Don't misunderstand! I know well and will forever embrace the truth of the cloud of witnesses, and I absolutely believe Jesus thoughtfully afforded our Josiah the best seat in the house via the heavenly realm that day, but nothing can change the effect of his physical absence in these pivotal moments on us all. Mind you, I wept for joy at each ceremony and danced the night away at each reception, but throughout was a knowing in our hearts that Josiah should have been there in the flesh.

Fast-forward to our precious grandchildren coming onto the scene. The Holy Spirit made sure that my heart was ready for a love explosion, but first He needed to address a wound so tucked away that I didn't even know it existed.

After Heather was wed, on occasion she and I would talk about grandkids. Again, because of our grief, we Bergers are extra careful with one another's hearts. We tend to overthink everyone's emotions. *How is this decision going to affect the kids' hearts? Is everyone going to be okay?* I don't doubt that at times we may be overly cautious with these concerns, but in the end, I think grieving families should ask for honest input from family members concerning major life decisions. Allow everyone a voice. Settle together on an answer that is closest to God's heart. Sometimes this requires *sacrifice* for the sake of preserving hearts. Sometimes it requires *courage* as God challenges us forward for the greater good to bring about change that in the moment may feel scary but makes for a new layer of strength and healing.

Here's an example. After her marriage, our daughter Heather would occasionally inquire, "Mom, will you be happy to be a grandma?" She was concerned about my heart and how I might handle it all. I think she could discern in my cool response that possibly I wasn't quite ready. I thought I was just being a groovy mom who wasn't pushing her adult children toward parenthood, like so many wannabe grandparents. But little did I know, deep in the recesses of my heart, there was a problem the Holy Spirit was preparing to touch. And true to His nature, His timing was perfect.

> Grieving families should ask for honest input from family members concerning major life decisions. Allow everyone a voice. Settle together on an answer that is closest to God's heart.

One night as I slept, the Lord visited me in a brilliant dream. I was standing and looking at a trap door on the roof of our house, like one you might find in an older home leading down into a basement. I grabbed its handle to pull the door open and peered down to see a ladder that led into the attic. Four rungs down, there was Josiah, at about three years old. My heart was filled with an emotion that I'd not known for years and had forgotten existed. Fellow mom, you know this feeling. It is that crazy love emotion you had when your babies were smaller and you sort of had a crush on them. Do you remember when your heart would swell at the thought of them? You just couldn't wait to hold them and squish them with all the love in your heart. Remember that? Well, that is how I felt.

I quickly shouted, "Josiah!" and with an excited calm, I climbed down those few rungs and held my little boy in my arms. In that moment I said, even within my dream, "This is a dream, and the Lord is telling me something!" Then I heard the Holy Spirit say to me, "Sarah, you will feel this way and much more when you're a grandmother." I immediately understood what He was working out in me.

When I awoke, the Lord continued to unfold all He intended for me to understand. First, the trap door into the roof of my house was symbolic of the hidden chambers of my heart—things He needed to show me in order to set me free.

Second, the Lord used Josiah to bring breakthrough because his absence was the immediate cause. The Lord had set me up! I was face to face with what I feared and questioned most. *Could I ever love another child? Could I ever risk giving my heart away so completely?* The casual approach I'd taken for years—the "no pressure" attitude toward grandchildren—was really birthed in fear.

Third, the Lord reminded me of what it felt like to love a child. It's an overwhelming emotion coupled with such joy. When He said, "You'll feel this way and more," He was, in His goodness, reminding me of how incredible it feels to love. He wanted me to remember that loving is well worth the risk, and I need not fear.

By the Lord's own hand, I was delivered from a fear I never realized I possessed. I woke the next morning free—ready for the future and all the grandchildren it might bring. So intimate are His ways.

Psalm 139:17–18 says, "How precious also are Your thoughts to me, O God! How great is the sum of them! If I should count them, they would be more in number than the sand; when I awake, I am still with You."

After receiving the gift of this dream, I knew the Lord was saying I needed to share this with Heather immediately. So, within a day, we sat together and I shared what the Lord had shown me. "Sis, I was afraid, and now I am not! Jesus wants you to know you don't have to be concerned about my heart, whether I will be okay or not. I am different. I am changed. I am excited!"

We wept together at the Lord's kindness—that He would so dearly walk this wounded family through life. He was taking His time to lead us through green pastures and to restore our very souls (see Ps. 23:1–3). Heather was free and I was free!

Two weeks after He visited me with this dream, Heather and Jarrett announced they were pregnant. In that moment, I was immediately shouting and jumping up and down for joy—sincere, beautiful joy! No doubt, my reaction would not have been as overwhelming apart from the deliverance God had just brought me through. Instead of being fearful and hesitant, I was ridiculously free and knew in my knower that I would love this child and every grandchild who followed. Not only that, but these children would awaken in me an indescribable joy, because He had said so!

Nine months later, our first grandchild was born: Trinity, or Trini, as we call her. She brought immediate, renewed excitement into my life. My children called me "baby hog" because I just couldn't get enough of her. I often approached anyone holding her and stole her away. What a fun time as family all gathered around Trini and watched her every move. She became our new live entertainment of sorts and truly has brought so much fun to our entire family!

Trini was followed by four other precious grandchildren, Maverick and Cohen (Cody and Keri's boys) and Haven and Shiloh (Heather and Jarrett's second and third daughters). This grandma just cannot wait to see their precious faces, and every time I do, I feel that "crush," that incredible love emotion the Lord reminded me of in my dream of deliverance. It is all true! He said I would feel this way and more as a grandma, and He was altogether spot-on.

He really is our mighty God, everlasting Father, Prince of Peace, and wonderful Counselor!

It's My Turn

For a few months before the decade anniversary of Josiah's exodus to Heaven, I was living with so much anger. Right under the surface, I was raging at nothing or no one in particular, but I felt a steady gnawing that found no resolve. I was so raw—not myself—as if I were living inside some person I didn't recognize. As I sat with the Lord day after day, asking, seeking, and knocking, I found no relief. I couldn't figure out what was going on.

My emotions were so uncharacteristic that my husband finally asked one day, "Honey, what is right under the surface?"

"Rage!" I replied. "Anger! I don't know the root, but I keep asking the Lord. I think I need to seek a counselor, because this is different. Not the blue of missing Josiah but a shadowboxing with something I can't see or recognize!"

While attending a night of worship at our church, I came forward to ask some ladies I knew and trusted for prayer. I confessed I was walking in anger and that it felt somehow connected to a control issue. I never imagined myself as a control freak, but I was falling into this trap. I confessed and they prayed. I don't even know what they prayed, but the next morning, as I sat reflecting with Christ, the answer came, lightning quick. *"Change!"* the Holy Spirit said, and in my knower, I understood.

"Change! Sarah, because of the devastating change you experienced ten years ago, you are resistant toward any change now—good or bad. You are fearful of the result and the sorrow that change brought into your life when Josiah left! Change gives birth to fear, and fear gives birth to rage."

I began to sob before the Lord. It all made sense, and although it was a painful truth, I wept with the relief of finally knowing what was going on in my soul. I told my husband what the Lord had said, and he held me in his arms while I convulsed in tears.

Several days later, I shared via text with my dear friend Kate what the Lord had revealed to me and the detail He continued to bring. She knows these deep places because one of her own children has also left for Heaven. As we texted and I exposed my heart, the Lord continued to speak His reasoning behind this difficult season.

> In my step-by-step journey through grief, the Lord has seen fit to press deep into my soul and spirit the knowing that my son is not only fine but far and above better than any of us living in the shadow of eternity.

I saw in my spirit a picture of Josiah standing alone, as though he was the center of attention. It wasn't a sad picture at all, only a statement: "Here is Siah. All eyes on him!" Then it was as if he was done, and now it was my turn. It reminded me of lining up for a license photo. His turn was over, and now it was mine—as if we were trading places. Kate literally texted this same thought as the Lord deposited it into my own heart. As if Josiah was saying, "I am good, Mom, and now it is your turn!"

The Holy Spirit has shown me that He, the God of *all* comfort, has been intent on answering all my intimate and at times bold questions about my son. He has been so willing to tend to my heart and woo me into asking some of the most outlandish questions—questions that our culture would deem irreverent. But He wanted to obliterate those walls, just as He tore the veil in the temple at Christ's death on the cross (see Matt. 27:50–52). He wants open dialogue, mom. Ask the hard questions and be fully honest with the God who knows all things. Nothing is hidden from Him.

Residue of Heaven

In my step-by-step journey through grief, the Lord has seen fit to press deep into my soul and spirit the knowing that my son is not only fine but far and above better than any of us living in the shadow of eternity. To know, figuratively speaking, that my child is safely tucked in at night—what mom's heart doesn't need that reassurance? He is experiencing a peace and joy that can never be stolen. He is never alone. Josiah is surrounded by the best of friends. He doesn't miss his friends and family here because in the Homeland, a day is as a thousand years and a thousand years as one day. Just a minute, and I will be there! No one can hurt my son's feelings or break his heart. He has food to eat, and he is safe. He lives in unity with all who surround him. He is experiencing a great adventure and is never bored. He is gleaning from the best! He is comrades with his own namesakes, King Josiah and King David. They are his friends, and I know he is fascinated by their stories of old.

> Josiah just got there sooner. Jesus is the forerunner of our faith, and Siah is the forerunner of our immediate family!

Best of all, Siah stands sure that Jesus *is* the King of Kings and Lord of Lords. Because of His death and resurrection and the entire Berger family trusting Christ for our salvation, we will all dwell one day in that same land. It will be better than it ever was before. All things will be redeemed. Heaven will make up for every sorrow. "Death, where is your sting?" (1 Cor. 15:55). Jesus has won the victory, and one day—I hope sooner rather than later—we will all be together again in the Kingdom, living the lives we have all been longing for. Josiah just got there sooner. Jesus is the forerunner of our faith, and Siah is the forerunner of our immediate family!

I long for the day when all hearts are perfectly in sync, and yet I know that in truth, this will only happen in the Kingdom. On occasion here on earth, there are those seasons, days, or moments when all feels so perfect and whole and happy. We call this foreshadowing of things to come the "residue of Heaven." We should all hold on to these moments tightly, remembering that there is a day coming when this will be our daily reality! Until then, may the Lord bait our lives with these moments, and may we all as fellow sojourners remain focused on the prize:

> Now I saw a new heaven and a new earth, for the first heaven and the first earth had passed away. Also there was no more sea. Then I, John, saw the holy city, New Jerusalem, coming down out of heaven from God, prepared as a bride adorned for her husband. And I heard a loud voice from heaven saying, "Behold, the tabernacle of God is with men, and He will dwell with them, and they shall be His people. God Himself will be with them and be their God. And God will wipe away every tear from their eyes; there shall be no more death, nor sorrow, nor crying. There shall be no more pain, for the former things have passed away."
>
> Then He who sat on the throne said, *"Behold, I make all things new."* And He said to me, "Write, for these words are true and faithful."
>
> And He said to me, "It is done! I am the Alpha and the Omega, the Beginning and the End. I will give of the fountain of the water of life freely to him who thirsts. He who overcomes shall inherit all things, and I will be his God and he shall be My son." (Rev. 21:1–7)

For this reason I bow my knees to the Father of our Lord Jesus Christ, from whom the whole family in heaven and earth is named, that He would grant you, according to the riches of His glory, to be strengthened with might through His Spirit in the inner man, that Christ may dwell in your hearts through faith; that you, being rooted and grounded in love, may be able to comprehend with all the saints what is the width and length and depth and height—to know the love of Christ which passes knowledge; that you may be filled with all the fullness of God.

Now to Him who is able to do exceedingly abundantly above all that we ask or think, according to the power that works in us, to Him be glory in the church by Christ Jesus to all generations, forever and ever. Amen. (Eph. 3:14–21)

Reflection

Sister, may I gently ask, how are your eyes? Are you seeing more clearly? Have you gained some eternal perspective? Some hope in *your* eleventh hour?

Now friend, I charge you as a fellow sojourner to share your own story. Make much of your loved one in the Kingdom. Speak his or her name. Live in the wonder of what he or she is doing in the land of the living. And in all of this, make *very* much of our Savior and King Jesus Christ, who gave His life that we might live!

For by Him all things were created that are in heaven and that are on earth, visible and invisible, whether thrones or dominions or principalities or powers. All things were created through Him and for Him. And He is before all things, and in Him all things consist. And He is the head of the body, the church, who is the beginning, the firstborn from the dead, that in all things He may have the preeminence. (Col. 1:16–18)

sarah's scrapbook

The Lord is close to the brokenhearted
PSALM 34:18

Wren by Liza Nicholson,
Sarah's sister (chapter 9)

Josiah trying
out military
gear (chapter 6)

The eagle
on our roof
(chapter 7)

Josiah with
his friend Lucy
(chapter 12)

Destiny and Heather in Hawaii (chapter 10)

Eagle by
Melissa
Townsend
(chapter 7)

Picking up Josiah's
Jeep on his birthday,
August 14, 2015
(chapter 12)

Josiah at graduation—in his Jeep (chapter 12)

Siah at Laguna Beach

Sarah
and
Siah

reflections

notes

introduction: josiah's story

1. "H7138 - qārôḇ - Strong's Hebrew Lexicon (NJKV)," under "Strong's Definitions," Blue Letter Bible, accessed April 12, 2022, www.blueletterbible.org/lexicon/h7138/nkjv/wlc/19-1.

chapter 2: it's about time

1. Lexico:.com, s.v. "importunity," accessed April 13, 2022, www.lexico.com/en/definition/importunity.

chapter 3: one body, one bread

1. W. E. Vine, *An Expository Dictionary of New Testament Words* (Nashville: Thomas Nelson, 1978), 46–47.

chapter 4: hidden manna

1. "4314. pros," under "Strong's Concordance," Bible Hub, accessed May 1, 2022, https://biblehub.com/greek/4314.htm.

2. There are a few other places in the Word where the term "asleep in Christ" is used. One example is 1 Corinthians 15:12–22, which speaks of the importance and truth of Christ's resurrection. I encourage you to read this passage aloud.

3. "4029. perikeimai," under "Strong's Concordance," Bible Hub, accessed April 13, 2022, https://biblehub.com/greek/4029.htm. See under "Strong's Exhaustive Concordance."

4. Randy Alcorn, *In Light of Eternity: Perspectives on Heaven* (Colorado Springs: Waterbrook, 1999), 2. Quotes are from the NIV.

5. "H5894 - `îr - Strong's Hebrew Lexicon (NKJV)," under "Strong's Definitions," Blue Letter Bible, accessed April 13, 2022, www.blueletterbible.org/lexicon/h5894 /nkjv/wlc/0-1; "H6922 - qadîš - Strong's Hebrew Lexicon (NKJV)," under "Strong's Definitions," Blue Letter Bible, accessed April 13, 2022, www.blueletterbible.org /lexicon/h6922/nkjv/wlc/0-1.

chapter 6: active duty

1. *NIrV Beginner's Bible*, Holy Bible: New International Readers Version (Grand Rapids: Zondervan, 1995, 2011), 1 Samuel 17:47.

chapter 7: the eagle

1. John Denver, "The Eagle and the Hawk," on *Aerie*, RCA Records, 1971, studio album.

2. "G5463 - chairō - Strong's Greek Lexicon (NKJV)," Blue Letter Bible, accessed April 14, 2022, www.blueletterbible.org/lexicon/g5463/nkjv/tr/0-1/.

3. *KJV Word Study Bible* (Nashville: Thomas Nelson, 2017), 1213.

chapter 8: occupy

1. *Merriam-Webster*, s.v. "occupy" (verb), accessed April 14, 2022, www.merriam -webster.com/dictionary/occupy.

chapter 10: the divine script

1. The "Gone Fishing" story originally appeared in and is adapted from our first book. See Steve and Sarah Berger, *Have Heart: Bridging the Gulf between Heaven and Earth* (Franklin, TN: Grace Chapel, 2010).

2. Alex Murashko, "Greg Laurie: People in Heaven Know What's Happening on Earth," *Christian Post*, July 30, 2012, www.christianpost.com/news /greg-laurie-people-in-heaven-know-whats-happening-on-earth.html.

3. "G1841 - exodos – Strong's Greek Lexicon (NKJV)," Blue Letter Bible, accessed April 14, 2022, www.blueletterbible.org/lexicon/g1841/nkjv/tr/0-1.

chapter 11: waves of reason

1. *Hitchcock's Bible Names Dictionary*, s.v. "Elihu," Bible Study Tools, accessed April 16, 2022, www.biblestudytools.com/dictionaries/hitchcocks-bible-names /elihu.html.

chapter 12: waves of change

1. Bethel Music and Amanda Lindsey Cook, "You Make Me Brave," by Amanda Lindsey Cook, on *You Make Me Brave*, Bethel Music, 2014, album.